Opening Texts

Opening Texts

USING WRITING TO TEACH LITERATURE

KATHLEEN DUDDEN ANDRASICK

Iolani School, Honolulu, Hawaii

With a Foreword by Thomas Newkirk

HEINEMANN *Portsmouth, New Hampshire*

Heinemann Educational Books, Inc.
361 Hanover Street Portsmouth, NH 03801-3959
Offices and agents throughout the world

Library of Congress Cataloging-in-Publication Data

Andrasick, Kathleen Dudden.
Opening texts : using writing to teach literature / Kathleen Dudden Andrasick : with a foreword by Thomas Newkirk.
p. cm.
Includes bibliographical references.
ISBN 0-435-08522-0
1. Language arts (Secondary) 2. English language—Composition and exercises—Study and teaching (Secondary) 3. Literature—Study and teaching (Secondary) I. Title.
LB1631.A55 1990
428'.0071'2—dc20 90-30045
CIP

Designed by Adrianne Onderdonk Dudden.
Printed in the United States of America.
90 91 92 93 94 9 8 7 6 5 4 3 2 1

For Jim,

and for Chris and Greg

Contents

Foreword

My connection with this book began with a seminar that I taught at the University of Hawaii, a seminar I never finished. Kathy Andrasick sat to my left, I remember, and became a virtual co-teacher. I asked each seminar member to write "responses," but she would bring in extended essays, week after week, that taught me more than most journal articles. For her final project she wanted to determine how ideas generated in small-group discussions in her class were adapted and integrated into students' final papers—a complicated project involving tape-recording, transcribing, and textual analysis.

I remember sitting in the university library, making notes for the last class, when someone came through the reading room saying, "Tsunami warning. Tsunami warning."

I turned to a student at my table. "What's a tsunami?"

"Tidal wave."

"What are they going to do about it?"

"Probably close down the university," she said, getting her books together.

Being from New Hampshire, I was, of course, more familiar with closings caused by snow. The university would announce that all "nonessential personnel" (and this would include faculty) should stay home. So we did. But I decided to get more guidance on tsunamis and went to the English department office.

"Should I cancel classes?" I asked.

"You bet. Tsunamis are serious business."

I decided to go to the class anyway to let people know it was cancelled. Kathy couldn't come—she had tsunami problems of her own. Bill Strong, who was visiting from Utah State and sitting in on the class, brought some freshly cut pineapples and, with a couple of other students, we sat on a patio and ate and talked as the tidal wave, triggered by an earthquake in the Aleutian Islands, moved our way.

At 4:30 the tsunami hit. It was three inches high.

Although Kathy Andrasick missed that last nonclass, we did have a chance to talk about her final project and to think ahead to this book. Often, in the very beginning stages, authors talk about writing "books," and you can almost hear the quotation marks. How can something no more material than an intention be called a "book"? But I never heard that tentativeness, those quotation marks, when Kathy talked about her book. In her acknowledgments she graciously gives me credit for "pushing" her toward this book. But, in truth, it was barely a nudge. From the moment she began graduate work she knew that she had something to say about enabling students to talk, read, and write critically.

F. Scott Fitzgerald has written (borrowing from Keats) that "the test of a first-rate intelligence is the ability to hold two opposed ideas in the mind at the same time, and still retain the ability to function." At the core of this book are two opposing ideas—or ideals—that the author seeks to reconcile. The first I will call the ideal of critical analysis, and the second the ideal of reader response.

The ideal of critical analysis is rooted in New Criticism, with its emphasis on close reading, formalism, the poem-as-object. A student writing about a poem should be able to explore the harmonious interconnection of elements, the pattern of images, the way form reinforces meaning. The personal reaction of the reader, the associations he or she might make, while not irrelevant, should not be equated with "the poem"—to do so is to commit the "affective fallacy." The critical analysis paper should be an argument for an interpretation supported by evidence from the text. One writing guide candidly states that the professor is not interested in "how" the interpretation came about—only in the plausibility of the interpretation itself. While a reader could, conceivably, apply this approach to any text, it seems best suited to complex works of art that would repay continual close readings.

Almost all advocates of the second ideal, that of reader response, begin with a rejection of this critical ideal. The act of reading, they claim, is not the objective perception of an aesthetic "object" but a transaction in which the reader "makes" a meaning that is not inherent in the object itself. The shaping influence of the reader is greater than the New Critics would have allowed. Women may well read differently than men; children differently than their parents; city dwellers differently than those raised in the country. The differences are inevitable and, in a democratic society, desirable.

The critical tradition, as applied to the classroom, left too many students by the wayside. Students were expected to adopt the formal style of argument without access to an informal language of exploration; they were expected to make bricks without straw. And almost any high school literature teacher knows the result—the empty, formulaic high school essay. For example, here is the way a student began his essay on religion in Maya Angelou's *I Know Why the Caged Bird Sings*:

> In the book *I Know Why the Caged Bird Sings* the theme of religion is found throughout the storyline. During the story religion is also involved in Maya's life and brought to her through her grandmother who she called "Mama."

The next paragraph, as you might expect, begins, "One example of religion. . . ." How much wasted energy is expended in writing these papers? How much time and effort in reading them?

The alternative offered by those advocating reader response usually stress what James Britton calls "expressive" discourse, language close to talk and gossip, language that can explore without having to assert, language that can *build* an interpretation. Nancie Atwell, in her acclaimed book *In the Middle*, shows how the exchange of letters can help students deepen their understanding of literature; Toby Fulwiler has shown the many uses of journals; and

Ann Berthoff has extended the idea of the basic journal to include "double entries" to allow students to comment on their observations. This list could go on for several pages.

The great virtue of *Opening Texts* is the way in which these two traditions are fused. Andrasick retains the best of the critical tradition—its high expectations, its emphasis on close reading and on the goal of sustained, thoughtful interpretations of literature. She also is an unapologetic advocate of requiring students to read major authors of some complexity—Joyce, Faulkner, Crane, Dickinson, and Hawthorne, to name a few. For this reason the book will appeal to the majority of English teachers who entered the profession because they loved these authors and who teach them in literature survey courses.

In a sense, then, *Opening Texts* is a conservative book. But it is also an innovative book. Andrasick draws on a rich array of exploratory strategies—classroom discussions, process logs, dialogue journals, and reading responses—that can help students work their way into literature. Through these forms of talk and writing, students make use of a language of exploration. In the section "Teaching Critical Distance," she shows how these early informal responses can be elaborated into extended pieces of analysis that do not resemble the empty formulaic writing of the canned school essay. Kathy Andrasick's achievement in this book is her unwillingness to treat reader response and critical analysis as competing ideals; she is able to view them as parts of a continuum, a progressive elaboration of meaning.

This is also a timely book. A recent report from the National Assessment of Educational Progress, *Learning to Be Literate in America*, attempts to redefine national goals for reading. The authors note that an overwhelming majority—approaching 100 percent—of students had attained a basic level of comprehension; they could derive a surface understanding from a variety of texts, and they could make basic generalizations. But they had real difficulty reasoning about what they read—analyzing, evaluating, and extending the ideas that are presented. Consequently, their first recommendation for change by teachers is for "depth of coverage":

> If students are to develop effective reasoning skills, they need to deal in depth with the materials they are reading and writing. Students need time to work on particular topics, and need thought-provoking questions from teachers and other students to help them as they refine and reformulate their initial understandings. It may be necessary to cover fewer topics to provide time for students to explore particular topics in more depth. (47)

It is precisely this attention to depth that readers will find in *Opening Texts*.

Thomas Newkirk

Acknowledgments

This book is the product of an intensely rewarding collaborative process that extended over many years. So many people share responsibility for its shape and its content that I can thank only a few directly.

First, I would like to thank my students. From them I learned what works and what doesn't in this business of education. They taught me the need to trust and believe in the validity of student responses to both procedures and materials. Their willingness to allow me to study and learn from their writing was gracious. Permitting me to collect that writing to share with other teachers has made this text possible.

My children taught me to be patient with the processes of maturation. In addition, from their generous tolerance of my shortcomings, I learned to tolerate those of my students. Christopher and Gregory taught me that students often have qualities and abilities that they rarely display in the classroom and caused me to seek ways to draw these hidden traits into the open.

Many of my own teachers shaped my thinking over a number of years. Most recently, I am grateful to Thomas Newkirk, who pushed me onto the path that led to this book, and to Jay Kastely, who taught me the importance of the ethical implications upon which it rests. I am also grateful to the many members of the English department at the University of Hawaii at Manoa, who shared their expertise and advice with me.

I am thankful to the colleagues with whom I have exchanged ideas and practice, including the many participants in the Hawaii Writing Project. I am lucky to know Mary Kay Masters, Diana Jones, and Beth Devereux, who constantly remind me that a generous stance toward students is the most productive. I am also grateful to those teachers who forced me over the years to consider my beliefs in light of their practice. This is a better book because it seeks to allay their potential dissent.

I am thankful, too, to David P. Coon, Headmaster of Iolani School, who allowed the leave of absence that made this book possible and then gracefully welcomed me back to a position on his faculty.

I am especially grateful to Ann Bayer of the College of Education and Walter Creed of the Department of English, both at the University of Hawaii at Manoa, who read generously and critically, offering me important responses to this work.

Joy Marsella, friend and mentor for the past eight years, has had perhaps the most influence on the shaping of this text. She encouraged me, prodded me, and directed me. She allowed me to define my project and gave me the intellectual room to create it. Her comments were honest and insightful; she read the early drafts both with me and against me. This is a better book than I could have written without her guidance, and I feel especially lucky to have had it.

Virginia Woolf insisted that writers need financial support and physical space. My husband Jim has provided both and so much more in addition that I cannot adequately express my gratitude. He believed in me and in the value of my work. He helped our children understand that there is importance in efforts that do not generate large paychecks. He did not complain about neglect, disorder, or despair, though he had to deal with all three. Without his encouragement, this book simply never would have been written.

To all of you, my thanks.

FUNDAMENTALS OF CRITICAL INQUIRY

1 Reclaiming the Range of Critical Discourse

I try not to spill coffee as I jostle my way in. The faculty mail room is always crowded on Monday morning.

Roger nods a greeting. "You've had Cynthia Shell in class before, haven't you?" he asks.

"Yes. Two years ago. Tenth grade." Roger looks disappointed. "Why?" I probe.

"Well, I just graded the first set of essays from that class, and hers was a real disappointment."

I tuck my grade book under my arm, shift the coffee cup to my left hand, and raise a quizzical eyebrow as I sort the contents of my mailbox.

"It has been an especially good class," he continues. "Their discussions of *The Scarlet Letter* were terrific. And Cynthia made some particularly insightful comments."

"And?" I deposit half the mail in the wastebasket as we leave the room.

"And their papers were all bad. Oh, they were mechanically fine. Beginnings, middles, and ends. Decent spelling. No big usage problems. But they were dull. Ordinary. Not a fresh thought in the group." He sighs, remembering his weekend, leaden with gray papers. "Cynthia's was especially disappointing, I guess. I *knew* she had interesting things to say, but she bored me to despair. It was like reading cold mashed potatoes—the instant ones. Blah."

"Cold mashed potatoes," I think, after we separate, heading toward our homerooms. I've had my share of those and dread them. The problem is that we just don't have the time to teach writing in our lit classes. It's hard enough to get through all the reading by June. Still, in addition to reading critically, students should be able to discuss the literature, both orally and in writing. We confront the perennial problem of all literature teachers: How can we help students learn critical inquiry and critical discourse without taking time from the literature that forms the core of our courses?

Roger's students have many useful critical skills, but, in spite of their ability to analyze texts and articulate observations, their writing lacks focus and voice. Yet Roger's class is in better shape than many. They, at least, know ways to talk about their literary encounters. What about the students who haven't learned to take the first steps toward critical discussion? Or those who don't have various strategies for engaging with texts and therefore read everything the same way? What about the students who are uncertain of their insights and timid about following observations with articulations? Worse, what about the ones whose literary readings remain superficial or tangential? If we wish to help students become skillful with critical inquiry, we may need to rethink our patterns of teaching literature. Although we mean well, our current pedagogical strategies may be less than helpful.

Typically, we ask students to read in isolation. Our questions and our suggestions regarding how they should focus their thinking are intended to give direction to their inquiry but may well close off other directions that students initiate alone. Rarely do we concentrate on teaching students *how* to compose meaning as readers.

Discussions of literature rarely engage all members of a group. Classes are too large. Some students don't do the reading. Shy students choose not to contribute. Whatever the reasons, even a lively, interesting discussion may not involve everyone. And those who are not fully involved in discussion may not be fully involved with the text, either.

Typically, when we ask students to write about their reading it is for an examination or a paper assignment. We *may* allow them to generate their own topics and help them do so. Often we don't. We *may* give them time to share drafts with trained peer groups and revise their papers. Often we don't. We use writing to evaluate our students—to judge their comprehension. That's fine. But what if we judge before we have taught strategies for both comprehension and composition? The resulting fare produced for our critical consumption is unappealing and bland; as with Roger's class, it may not even represent student capabilities properly.

All readers—sophisticates and neophytes—make personal, idiosyncratic connections with texts before they do much else. Initially, such connections may be quite simple: "I like this," or "This is boring," or "I don't understand this poem." A connection may relate a reader's personal experience to the text: "Pip's love for Estella reminds me of when I was in love with the prettiest girl in the eighth grade and she wouldn't dance with me." Finally, a personal connection may contain the initial germ of a useful critical insight: "Hawthorne writes about a lot of ministers."

Coupled with personal connection is the composition of an initial understanding of a text. A reader begins to use personal language to make a coherent—although not necessarily complete—statement about the text. Again, such statements vary widely in sophistication. They may be as simple as "This is a book about dogs" or as critically astute as "Hawthorne uses ambiguity and the density of the forest in 'Young Goodman Brown' to suggest the difficulty of penetrating an individual psyche."

A critical reader must be able to distance self from text, to change and/or enlarge the angle of vision in order to probe a text for useful and meaningful observations and, eventually, to question it. For students, this distancing is fraught with danger and the risk of failure. How can they, mere beginners after all, hope to say anything useful or intelligent about, for example, Shakespeare? Don't teachers already know all the smart things that can be said about *Macbeth?*

As literature teachers, the core of our enterprise is first to help students recognize and *value* their personal connections and initial readings. Next, we must help them acquire the strategies that foster critical inquiry. The dialogue journals, process logs, and reading responses I describe in chapters 3, 4, and 5 enable personal connection and perception, and encourage recognition of worth. The focus is on reading, writing, and talking as tentative, exploratory, and creative interwoven processes of experiencing texts and composing meanings.

Engaging in critical inquiry means learning how to question texts. Questioning texts demands critical distance. Chapters 6 and 7, "Imitating and Transforming Texts," and "Transforming and Acquiring Texts," work obliquely to teach students to establish that distance. Students learn to oppose textual authority by becoming conscious of the ways in which textual language imposes such authority. The critical problems we offer for practice allow student experimentation with texts. That experimentation in turn empowers subsequent freedom of critical inquiry.

Initially, writing and talking help students compose their readings of literary texts. Later, as a class works collaboratively to broaden its understandings of a text, writing enables and formalizes literary discussion among students and between student and teacher. Because reading, writing, and talking are reciprocal and parallel uses of language to compose meaning, they should be integrated, not separated, as we focus our attention on critical inquiry.

In such a context, critical discourse (written and spoken) helps students:

- Explore literature for questions and insights interesting to them.
- Compose meanings from texts.
- Know how they understand literature and expand the repertory of ways they compose meanings from texts.
- Make connections between and among texts.
- Learn to trust their responses and critical assessments.

- Enjoy literature on levels beyond simple comprehension of narrative line.

Students need constant practice to develop into capable, functioning adults in a verbally complex society. In a literature classroom, this means practice in approaching language (a literary text) through language (their own talking and writing). It means practice in generating, testing, and presenting critical observations to a real audience.

However, at the high-school and college levels, our training often leads us to neglect such practice. Instead, we tend to substitute artificial exercises for real language use. Schools stop teaching reading skills, per se, after students leave the elementary level, yet advanced reading strategies are fundamental to literary encounters. Furthermore, classroom discussions are often not discussions at all. In the proper sense of the word, a discussion is a conversation in which peers share ideas and observations, mutually exploring a subject. Yet, in many literature classrooms, such conversations often degrade into artificial performances during which teachers ask preformulated questions designed to see how much students have figured out about a text.

The writing students do in our classrooms can become equally artificial. Typically, we ask a student to write a critical argument based on a text. The form itself demands that the student has already accomplished a coherent reading of the text and precludes explorations of what is confusing—the inconsistencies and what Thomas Newkirk calls "the possibilities of the incoherencies" (1990, 210). For many students, however, unexplored or unresolved incoherencies still constitute a dominant portion of their responses to a text at the time when we ask them to assume a critical role. Instead of using incoherencies as points of critical departure, students neglect questions the text raises in their rush to act critically, blinding themselves to possibilities as they seek convenient theses. They narrow the terrain of their reading, ignoring all but the most dominant physical features. Because they envision such limited landscapes, their compositions become bland and predictable.

As teachers of literature, we are often ill trained to use writing as a tool for teaching and learning. We concentrate on formal products to the exclusion of other kinds of writing. We mark mechanical problems on finished papers but ignore (or don't know how to approach) issues of form and content that arise during the composing process. Instead of presenting real conventions of critical discourse—and instruction in its production—we offer an inadequate and limited form for student use. Our pedagogical shortcomings are directly reflected in the quality of the writing our students produce about their reading.

Writing has the power to generate thinking and to enable connections, thereby creating new relationships; teachers in literature classes thus can use writing to teach literature. We can offer writing opportunities that broaden students' understandings of individual texts and of modes of composing meaning. We can use writing to expand student perception and exploration of texts. Through writing, students can attain critical distance from texts.

Using writing as more than a means of evaluation is imperative for teachers who seek to develop independent learners. Students must be given control over all aspects of their work. As they take full responsibility for their composing as readers, they learn how readers make meaning, how texts instruct readers to compose, and the ways in which both readers and texts are culturally bound. When students take full responsibility for their composing as writers, they learn to use writing to shape real meaning in response to complex questions. By extension, they develop a power to use language applicable to a multitude of real-life situations.

When we include writing in our collaborative model of critical inquiry, we put pressure on traditional assumptions regarding the appropriate audience for student writing. Arthur Applebee's study of student writing in high school (1981) reveals that, in all subjects, the most common audience for student writing is the teacher-as-examiner. However, teachers who want students to develop into competent, fully participating members of a literary discourse community must forgo this central role. Instead, we must provide opportunities for students to respond to, comment on, and evaluate the critical discourse of their classmates and make these opportunities a central part of the natural and ongoing critical conversations of our classrooms.

Teachers concerned about sharing or abdicating their examining role need not worry. Researchers recognize the central importance of audience to composing, agreeing that mature writers are able both to imagine and invoke the ever-changing variety of audiences appropriate to an ever-changing variety of rhetorical situations (Berkenkotter 1981; Ede and Lunsford 1984; Kroll 1984). Indeed, a writer's mental image of a particular audience is a fundamental component of his or her writing process; decisions regarding content, organization, and style are made in response to this audience's hypothetical readings. As students gain experience writing for a diversity of potential audiences, they become more skillful writers.

A collaborative classroom enriches students' sense of audience to include not only actual readers but all who influence the writer during the process of composition, including, of course, the writer as reader of his or her own text. Balancing the constantly shifting relationships between writer and reader is a complex process requiring extensive practice; such practice is more easily experienced in a collaborative classroom than in a teacher-centered one.

In his study, Applebee also suggests that, paradoxically, writing for a teacherly audience typically "requires *less writing skill* [emphasis added] than virtually any other audience" (1981, 51). Teachers read for content, are willing to fill in gaps, and are experienced enough to adjust for the semantic confusions found in student texts. By assisting student writers in these ways, teachers deny them access to both the frustrations and the satisfactions of real reader response. Students need to experience the difficulties of shaping words to convey clear meaning to many other sensibilities, as well as the pleasure of receiving appropriate responses to their written language.

Like all communication, writing is fundamentally social, and one of the central processes students must learn is decentering—moving beyond their egocentrism to consider the needs and responses of others. The persistence of egocentrism is a flaw with which teachers are all too familiar in student writing. Students need to experience the social interactions of the writer-reader relationship to overcome such egocentrism. Practice with varied feedback helps them develop an intuitive sense of audience to suit varying compositional needs. Activities fundamental to the collaborative classroom—collaborative writing, pair sharing, peer-response groups, and literary discussions based on student writing—naturally work to broaden audience conception.

Stilted, formulaic student writing is due in part to a notion left over from the seventeenth and eighteenth centuries: a belief in an unchanging universe where all knowledge can be described in positivistic terms and where preexisting "Truth" can be apprehended by logical, reasonable scientific inquiry.

This world view is innate in two classroom assumptions: (1) if a reader studies a text long enough and skillfully enough, its "meaning" will become apparent; and (2) if a writer thinks hard enough and logically enough, he or she will be able to produce a single assertion—"the thesis"—for a topic. These two common assumptions are particularly insidious because, when modified somewhat ("a text may have several meanings if each is consistent with the others," or "a topic might produce several assertions as long as each can be proved"), they mask the philosophy in which they are rooted. And, so masked, they appear less alien than they really are to twentieth-century understandings shared in many disciplines about the nature of human thought, language, and the making of meaning.

In the twentieth century, language is understood to be neither neutral nor directly referential. In *Thought and Language,* Vygotsky writes, "the relation of thought to word is not a thing but a process.... Thought is not merely expressed in words; it comes into existence through them" (1986, 218). Meanings are contingent upon the language available for expression. Direct equivalency of words and experience, of words and reality, is impossible. Furthermore, thought, language, and meaning are always contextually bound. An objective, quantifiable, nonreferential *meaning* becomes impossible.[1]

Unfortunately, many writing texts and assignments do not encourage or allow students to come to new meanings. Instead, they remain grounded in a paradigm that emphasizes product, views discourse only in terms of description, narration, exposition, and argument, is intensely concerned with usage and style, is preoccupied with the thesis-driven essay and the research paper, and assumes that *composing* as a process cannot be taught (Hairston 1982, 78).

David Bartholomae notes that this "peculiar rhetoric of the composition class"—and, I wish to claim, of the literature class—is obsessed with the notion of the thesis or controlling idea. He further suggests that "the tyranny of the thesis often invalidates the very act of analysis we hope to invoke" (1983, 311). Such writing limits a subject and so limits the potential for a conversation evolving from it. In fact, many writing texts ignore the idea of critical *conversation* as they privilege the thesis-driven essay in which a student is exhorted to "prove" something interesting, or "argue convincingly" about an aspect of a text.[2] The assumption is that writers know what to express before the writing begins and that all they need do is summon what they already know.[3] As a result, academic writing about literature is often stilted, formulaic, and lacking in human conviction or voice. It reads like cold mashed potatoes partly because it equates critical discourse with argument rather than with exploratory dialectic.

This "peculiar rhetoric"—the conventional thesis-driven argument paper—provides limited satisfaction as a tool for critical inquiry because it requires the writer to assume a controversial position to defend logically. The reductiveness of the form is self-evident. "Thesis" suggests an assertion, and single assertions suggest single points of view; the form ignores all the potential attitudes between "yes" and "no."

The world presents too many useful possibilities for us to structure it into systems of mutually exclusive absolutes. It is time to change our emphasis. Although historically established, the thesis-driven argument essay does not merit its privileged position either in terms of how humans think or in terms of how critical inquiry can productively be taught and expressed. Ultimately, the focus on thesis and argument limits our students' understanding of what writing can and should do. A great deal of literary exploration is potentially available that a thesis-limited argument is incapable of addressing successfully.

A collaborative classroom shifts students from an argumentative stance to a dialectical relationship with their texts and with one another. They consider all the ways texts might touch them as readers or that they might touch a text. They extend their collaboration to include the interactions among all readers of a text who are generous enough to share insights.

Such interactions have implications concerning the shape of discourse that we deem appropriate for critical explorations. Given the tentative nature of critical conclusions within a collaborative context, the traditionally unquestioned notion of beginning-middle-end might well be reconsidered. We must be clear that "end" means *an* end, not *the* end, as in fairy tales. Endings need to be understood as potential new beginnings for new enterprises.[4]

We no longer ought to ask students that they limit themselves to the traditional linear form, diagramed by many teachers and composition texts like this:

Introduction
Point 1
Point 2
Point 3
Conclusion

Such a diagram is well intentioned; instructors mean to help students visualize the different parts of a paper and what each is supposed to do. However, the diagram suggests an unnecessarily elementary form, insisting as it does that synthetic order is always the best pattern of development.

This pattern is easy to teach and easy to learn. Our clever, obedient students come to use it almost mechanically. However, most writers have difficulty maintaining reader interest after they reveal the "main point" in the first paragraph. By contrast, a writer who takes a more exploratory stance flexibly shapes content to suit purposes and generate reader interest. Such a writer may have to work harder to forge and connect a complex chain of assertions, but the sophistication of such analytic arrangements more properly reflects the complexities of literary analysis. Real discussions typically assume analytic forms that are untidy and diffuse.

Teachers must take scrupulous care to assert the organic relationships between content and form. We must categorically deny the absolute validity of any one form, no matter how theoretically elegant. Classroom discussions should properly come in many sizes and shapes; sometimes, these will not be what we think of as conventional. That is precisely as it must be. The traditional emphasis in our classrooms has been artificially narrow. We are ready for expansion.

While we are reconsidering form, I wish to reinclude those forms we classify as creative writing in our critical discourse. All composition is creative. The distinction between creative writing and expository writing is ill defined and ill labeled at best. Drama, poetry, and fictional narrative all have value as ways of teaching critical inquiry, yet we have often dismissed them from our literature classrooms as inappropriate. Creative forms, which provide us with imaginative ways to apprehend and shape experience, have enormous potential as a supplement to conventional critical discourse; their dramatic nature bridges oppositions and empowers synthesis.

As we train students in critical inquiry, we must provide them with writing opportunities that are real—that is, with a real communicative purpose and a real audience ready and interested in receiving the communication. Too often, the assignments we give students are only exercises, irrelevant to their lives, their work, or their literary communities. They have little meaning. Unhappily, after years of doing such exercises, students conceptualize writing as writing exercises, thinking of it as something they do only in an English class.

Not only must assignments be real, they must be connected. Isolated assignments are like recipes. They work and may be useful, but their value is limited by isolation. Alone, they cannot teach the principles of omelets, or of sauce making, for example. Writing activities done out of context are prone to trivialization. When supported by a progressive sequence of experiences, however, they move students toward increased intellectual and critical power. We do ourselves and our students a disservice when we do not plan assignments in sequences.[5]

In the past, literature instruction was product centered. Influenced by the insights of New Criticism, teachers saw texts spatially, as things to be moved through, left to right, top to bottom, front to back. Such a view sees only the text and ignores the reader. It minimizes aesthetic experiences by focusing only on aesthetic objects.

In recent years, both the traditional forms of discourse and our view of literature have been challenged. Teachers are becoming uncomfortable with a product-centered pedagogy in both reading and writing. Learning is not merely collecting facts, gathering an aggrandizement of data, a movement from not knowing the capitals of France or Egypt to knowing they are Paris and Cairo. Learning is thinking; it is using prior knowledge and thinking strategies to understand, to make meaning. Learning is connecting and organizing information; it is goal oriented and influenced by the learner's developmental level; it is nonlinear.

As our definition of learning expands beyond the acquisition of data to include ways of operating with information—strategies and procedures for processing and using information—we can no longer see ourselves simply as information givers. Such a view both overemphasizes the transmission and fails to account for the reception; it overemphasizes the information and neglects the potential manipulation of that information. We should no longer view students as empty vessels to be filled with facts but as community members who operate linguistically in a complex and rapidly changing society. We should no longer assume that mechanical, formally correct, artificial discourse is all students are capable of producing. As teachers, we want students to generate something legitimate to read. But, if we demand higher standards, we will need to change our teaching. We need to think of teaching both the content and the strategies that the content requires. We must learn to think of our teaching in terms of providing students *ex-*

periences with content and then helping them recognize and understand the lessons embedded in those experiences. Teachers must begin to deal with both product (information) and process (ways of learning and using information).

2 Enabling Critical Conversation

Literature teachers might take comfort from Herman Melville. He tells us, "there are some enterprises in which a careful disorderliness is the true method." A successful literature classroom depends upon careful disorder. Plans must be scrupulously careful. Student skills, abilities, and needs must be considered. A wide range of language experiences must be designed. Challenging texts must be explored. However, it is impossible to teach students how to approach and discuss texts critically in a formulaic, step-by-step fashion. The enterprise and our true method are both too complex.

Disorder, however, makes us uncomfortable. We worry about accountability and classroom control. These concerns often shape our pedagogy. As Peter Elbow suggests, "much teaching behavior stems from an unwarranted fear of things falling apart" (1986, 71–72). A classroom centered around the teacher dispensing wisdom and information, then evaluating student assimilation of that information, feels like a quiet, safe place to work, a place where nothing can fall apart. And it is—for the teacher, who is in control, who knows exactly what will happen next and how, because he or she is making it happen.

It is not such a safe place for students, however. They are being directed by forces over which they have no control (the teacher, the text, and the curriculum, for example). Furthermore, they have little or no control over classroom events, not even over the topic of discussion or its direction. For students, things often fall apart. They encounter surprise quizzes, questions they have never considered and for which they have no answers, and tasks for which they have had little or no training. At school, they confront the risk of embarrassment and failure hourly. We should not need to be told that the tension and discomfort (and perhaps fear) that students feel deflect their attention from learning. Common sense tells us that the context we create for students affects their thinking; classroom context can limit as well as empower learning.

The least efficient, least effective way to teach critical inquiry is through exclusive (or extensive) use of teacher talk. While this mode of instruction may provide students with information about a particular lecture topic, it fails to teach them the processes in which the lecturer is skilled: reading texts, generating material for comment, and shaping that material for public presentation. Experience insists that students do not learn how to do something by being told how; they learn by practice. It follows that productive literature classes are those that provide maximum opportunities for students to experience and engage with texts: to discover, explore, and reflect. Productive literature classes also work to expand students' repertoires of strategies for discovery, exploration, and reflection. They give students repeated critical experiences with literature and then help them reflect on those experiences.

The teacher must become a participator in conversation as much as its director. Teachers must read and talk and write with students (although not necessarily about the same texts, if that becomes artificial). Teacher participation not only provides a model for students to follow, it insists on the validity and meaningfulness of the activities in which the community is engaged. Reading literature, and talking and writing about it, are legitimate activities, not just for apprentices but for professionals.

In collaborative classrooms, the teacher (and the curriculum) establishes a content framework, but the students are responsible

SEPTEMBER 8 *monday*

Wisdom is the principal thing; therefore get wisdom.
And in all your getting, get understanding.

Proverbs 4:7 (NKJV)

for the order and the direction in which the content is assimilated. As a result, much of the tension is eased, and learning is empowered. Unfortunately, collaborative classrooms sometimes feel disorderly to a teacher, who may equate lessened control over educational process with reduced educational product.

Teachers fear that when students make choices in the classroom and control the direction of discussion they learn less. They worry about standards and a loss of rigor. So do I. However, while teachers directing collaborative classes give up knowing the exact order in which things will happen, they do not give up identifying what students need to learn. At the same time, students find such classes to be safer, more reasonable, and more productive places because they have a central role in the direction of their own learning.

I begin my courses with two classroom activities that are models of Melville's "careful disorderliness." On the first day or two of a course, I ask students to explore the text (if we are using an anthology) or texts (if we will be reading several works). I ask them to find something interesting to read that they have not read before, to read it for twenty to thirty minutes, and to come to class the next day prepared to share their findings by presenting a brief summary and/or commentary on what they read and by reading a short passage aloud.

We spend several class periods with everyone (including me) sharing. (If I have already read everything in the class texts, I read something new—but related—rather than participate artificially.) The sharing order varies; often, two people will have read the same (or a similar) selection, and one may offer to extend the observation and commentary of the classmate. After each reading, I attempt to highlight, contextualize, and make connections among the different texts. I use this time to indicate the themes or patterns that we will encounter throughout the course. I begin to set up the framework and develop the outlines within which we will work.

This activity accomplishes many things. First, it demystifies the course content. Students develop a sense of what is in their books and the demands that will be made on them as readers. Typically, they discover that intimidating exteriors (especially the bulky anthologies that are used in many of our survey courses) hide accessible interiors. Each has found something interesting, and each has been directed to other readings of potential interest by peers.

In addition, this activity establishes the group relationships central to our work throughout the course. Every individual has the opportunity to speak to the group as an expert, sharing his or her understandings. Each individual benefits, in turn, from the expertise of others. The teacher is cast in the same roles, both sharing and receiving expertise. Underlying the enterprise is the assumption that collaborative language functions (externally, as in talking and writing, and internally, as in listening and reading) as a fundamental tool for textual exploration.

A second useful, but disorderly, activity also demonstrates the value of collaborative language use and reinforces the importance of the plurality of views accessible in a literature classroom. When introducing the first text we will read together as a group, I take ten minutes of a class period and ask students to read and mark anything they notice that seems important to them. (I am assuming that students buy their own books; if that is not the case, the same point can be made by photocopying several pages of a common text for students to mark.)

Again, we go around the room, with students telling what they marked. I wonder why some students have underlined entire sentences and others only single words. I ask students why they used brackets or asterisks or check marks. I ask them to explain why they marked certain things. Sometimes they can ("It was the name of a character; I wanted to remember it"), but often they cannot.

The diversity of annotation is quickly evident, both in terms of volume and content. When the sharing is finished, I emphasize that diversity by noting, "Everybody did this differently." I ask, "Who did it right?" They quickly see that each textual response, while idiosyncratic, is correct and learn to accept the individual, intuitive nature of their textual markings—their noticings. I point out that the function of group discussion—of critical collaboration—is to enable the class to benefit from the *range* of observations, both to experience a particular text more fully and to learn new patterns of textual observation.

This discussion also provides me with an early way to observe and analyze my students' textual strategies. My notes on their responses are not limited to content but include as much as I can ascertain about their methodology. With a new group of students, opportunities for early assessment are invaluable.

Both these activities provide students with particular literary experiences and provide me with multiple teaching opportunities. I have an agenda, but the order in which I teach items (and, indeed, sometimes the items themselves, when discussion reveals gaps in student skills or understanding) emerges from student experience rather than being previously determined by me. If a particular issue is neglected or omitted altogether, I plan another experience that will bring it into the foreground. I have time. We will work together for a semester or a year. The key issues and strategies will arise again and again, and what is ignored during one class session can become central in others.

I am suggesting we adopt a classroom context that more nearly approximates the ways in which people work and learn outside the academy, a context that is collaborative and social. There are excellent reasons for doing so, as cooperative learning increases academic achievement and enhances student learning and thinking.

Collaboration provides emotional support; the group becomes a resource for each individual. Collectively, the group has more information and a keener critical facility than any single member. Collaboration demonstrates the truth of the old saw that the whole is greater than the sum of its parts. Group members validate and clarify understanding and judgments for one another.

Collaboration forces confrontation with new points of view and provides students opportunities to evaluate, analyze, and compare a variety of observations. As the group works, individuals become aware of factors that influence judgments; presented with varied opinions and evaluation strategies, students are better able to consider alternatives and less likely to feel compelled to accept the first idea presented. They have to evaluate various positions in order to determine their own. They learn to rethink and perhaps revise their initial readings. They learn new questions to ask, and they grow as critics because, as Peter Elbow suggests, "the crucial mental event in growth is often the *abandonment* of a position we hold" (1985, 289). Group learning makes such abandonment both more possible and more tempting as students transcend the initial limitations of private response.

Students have opportunities to rehearse concepts and strategies when they work collaboratively. Learning is optimized because students can test ideas, with the group providing immediate feedback. Students construct frameworks of information that interweave through collaboration to form a web of literary knowledge.

Collaborative learning also engenders growth in thinking abilities. Group validation of specific, concrete information enables the individual to reconceptualize the material in general terms. Collaboration supports conceptual validation and expansion as well. Students learn ways of perceiving as they learn ways of judging. They internalize the thoughts and thinking strategies of their peers and, in doing so, become more autonomous learners.

The classroom model that I describe here and that returns in every chapter of this book is designed explicitly to provide such a collaborative context in which students can learn the principles of critical inquiry. The course structure forces students to take primary responsibility for their own textual explorations. It leads them to generate and address questions that become real concerns for them. It seeks to induct them as members in a club of critical inquirers, participants in a critical community engaged in energetic and thoughtful reading and discussion of texts.

Enabling students to reach full membership in a critical community is a demanding teaching endeavor and can only be accomplished over time. Learning takes place when students are actively involved, when the situation provides emotional support, when students practice an analytic attitude and experiment with new concepts, and when they receive prompt feedback for their newly developed ideas. It requires a context for learning that is productive and comfortable for students, so that they will feel both motivated and positive about their efforts. Let me describe my plan for teaching *The Red Badge of Courage* as an example of how such a learning context can be created.

I have several aims for this teaching segment, which comes about halfway through a traditionally ordered American literature course. Naturally, I want students to read and understand the book on a literal level. In addition (as might be expected), I use the text to help students understand the assumptions and implications of Naturalism. Furthermore, I want the class to continue its explorations (begun earlier with Hawthorne) of the ways in which different authors develop characters in extended narrative. Because we have already looked at imagery and how it works in poetry, I also like to take the opportunity to introduce students to the ways patterns of imagery provide connections throughout an extended narrative. Finally, working within the context of the formal paper that students write on the novel, I introduce students to some effective ways of using material quoted directly from a literary text.

The time constraints of the curriculum give us only seven class periods for work on the novel. I must plan extremely carefully, because I don't want simply to cover the book. I have learned to plan such units considering both product and process. I divide my thinking into *what* I will teach—the content—and *how* I will teach—the activities and assignments students will experience—and *how* I will evaluate both knowledge and performance. I make three lists. First, I list my objectives—what I wish students to learn. Next, I list my procedures—the activities, exercises, and assignments designed to meet the objectives. These two lists show at a glance if I have built in a sufficient variety of language experiences and managed a mix of support and feedback with independent performance. Finally, I list evaluation tools appropriate to the unit. This list properly separates teaching from evaluation and also reminds me that I may wish to evaluate *before* I am ready to grade—at the beginning of a unit, for example, if I wish to see what students already know.

Here are my three lists for teaching *The Red Badge of Courage.*

LIST 1: Objectives

- Students should understand the novel on a literal level (they should be able to recall characters, major plot events, and settings).
- Students should learn and be able to apply to the book an accessible definition of Naturalism.

- Students should learn to trace a repeated image through an extended work.
- Students should learn to question a repeated image for patterns and emerging meanings.
- Students should learn to choose and use quoted material properly for effective illustration in analytical writing.

LIST 2: Procedures

- Students will carry out "Yes-I-read-the-book" writing and class discussion.
- Students will look up and bring to class a definition of Naturalism. We will use class discussion to clarify and simplify that definition. Students will work in groups to find expressions of that philosophic position in the text. Group findings will be shared with the class.
- Students will trace a particular image through the novel; they will work in groups to validate and extend their findings. They will analyze and report to the class the significance of any patterns they notice. They will repeat this process independently, using a new image, in papers that they will share with the class.
- They will read a handout on using quoted material effectively. They will practice using quotations in their imagery paper.

LIST 3: Evaluation

- "Yes-I-read-the-book" writing and my record of class discussion.
- Written homework checks and my record (informal) of group participation.
- Final unit essay in which students discuss an image not covered by class work and show how the image relates to the work as a whole. The writing should display appropriate choice and use of quoted material.

Having planned the what and the how of a unit, I am ready to determine the when. The daily schedule for this particular unit looks like this:

- *Day 1*: "Yes-I-read-the-book" writing. (Here I am evaluating what students know as we begin work.) Discussion of Henry's shattered expectations (based on writing).

- *Day 2*: Group work on characters; character reports. Class discussion of flat and round characters.
- *Day 3*: Discussion of Jim Conklin as a character who changes. Discussion of his death scene and its impact. Discussion of Henry Fleming and his changes, and discussion of the experiences centrally connected to those changes.
- *Day 4*: Defining Naturalism, and sharing and testing representative passages.
- *Days 5 and 6*: Group work on imagery and reports to class. Discussion of how the imagery works in this text.
- *Day 7*: Wrap up discussion. Mini-lesson on using quoted material effectively. Paper assignment given (drafts are due in several days; class time is allotted to peer response and editing).

Before I describe in detail what happens on each day of the unit, I cannot resist digressing momentarily to argue against a teaching strategy that I abhor on both critical and pedagogical grounds: having students read and discuss a novel in chapter segments. Such an approach may be forgivable for a work as complex as Joyce's *Ulysses* and understandable when the intention is to give students a serial experience of a novel that was originally published in serial form (such as Dickens's *Bleak House*), but there are few other excuses for it. A novel is an artistic whole and deserves to be experienced as such. Remembering Ford Madox Ford's observation that, in the last lines of a narrative, a "lightening flash is thrown back over the whole story and all its parts fall into place" (quoted in Miller 1968, 160), it seems only sensible to allow readers the benefit of full illumination before asking for critical commentary.

From a pedagogical point of view, the chapter-by-chapter approach too often degrades into deadly daily plot summary. Think what cannot be done with the segmented approach: students cannot trace lines of imagery or symbolism through a text as a whole, focus discussion on repeated structures (such as the three scaffolding scenes in *The Scarlet Letter* or the three stages of Pip's expectations), search for parallel or repeated events with an eye to their transformations, or deal with character development except in a piecemeal fashion. A segmented approach spoon-feeds lazy students unnecessarily; it bores and handicaps good readers. Finished with a book long before the discussion is over, good readers are unreasonably limited in their comments by a fear of revealing material from later chapters that classmates have not yet read.

Furthermore, talking about a text in little bits takes more class time than talking about a text as a whole. Students who discuss a novel in its entirety get more done, more thoroughly, than students in classes with a fragmented approach.

I am stepping off my soap box. We can now begin to trace how my outline translates into actual activity in the classroom.

Students come to class on the first day of the unit having already read the book and having written for a half hour in response to their reading. (See chapter 5 for a detailed discussion of the reading response and its uses.) This response writing is designed to help students make the first connections with the text and prepare them for discussion. Further, it provides me with a reading check. Students simply cannot write a reading response without reading!

Yes-I-read-the-book writing is the first in-class unit activity. I use this label because, as I tell the students, if they faithfully read the whole book, they will be able to do well with the task. I use this writing in several ways: (1) to give students an opportunity to demonstrate that they read the book and get credit for that reading; (2) to give me a tool with which to evaluate the quality of their readings; and (3) to provide a starting point for class discussion. The directions are as follows:

▬ *THE RED BADGE OF COURAGE*

One critic of *The Red Badge of Courage,* R. W. Stallman, writes: "Everything goes awry; nothing turns out as Henry had expected" (1976, 201).

Identify and define as many of Henry's expectations about war, himself, and his behavior as you can, and briefly detail how these expectations go awry. Be sure to comment on Henry's feelings at the end of the novel.

Circulating around the room while students write, I can tell who has finished the reading and who has not. Any offenders I send to the library with a long (and boring) study guide or research question connected to the text, which they are to complete before returning to class. The message is that *not* doing the reading is more work than doing it! Recidivism is rare—in fact, the message is so thoroughly absorbed by the class that, after our first novel, it is the unusual student who fails to complete the reading on time.

At the end of twenty minutes or so, we begin discussion by having several students read aloud while we make lists of the expectations that are shattered by Henry's experience. Once the class has generated a rich listing, I ask them to consider the implications of having expectations gone awry emerge as a central issue in the text. Because of the scope of the question, discussion ranges throughout the novel and gives us the opportunity to clarify misunderstandings held by individual students while we grapple with a central theme.

Perhaps my most basic discussion strategy is to say as little as possible. First, I am too busy keeping a record of the discussion—no easy task. Not only must I remember what was said, I must recall who said it! When I teach several sections of the same course, I often find myself wondering if I heard a certain comment during period 5 or period 7. To combat these difficulties, I have learned to use my seating plan. I make photocopies for each day's discussion, on which I summarize each student's contributions as he or she speaks. Sometimes, only a word or two is necessary to remind me of the origin of a key point. Figure 2–1 shows a sample record of a discussion one class had of Katherine Ann Porter's "Flowering Judas." Clearly, such notes are fragmented and unclear to anyone except the participants. Still, they are enough to remind me of the pattern of a discussion several weeks later. Further, because I am busy with this note taking, often I am not looking at the speakers. This lack of eye contact with me forces students to look at (and speak to) each other.

When I do speak, I help students link their comments to what others have said. I help them shape questions and articulate their observations as precisely as possible. I offer as few explanations and as little information as I can. I turn every question back to the group for consideration. Some of my frequent responses are "What do *you* think about that?" "What else do we know about that?"

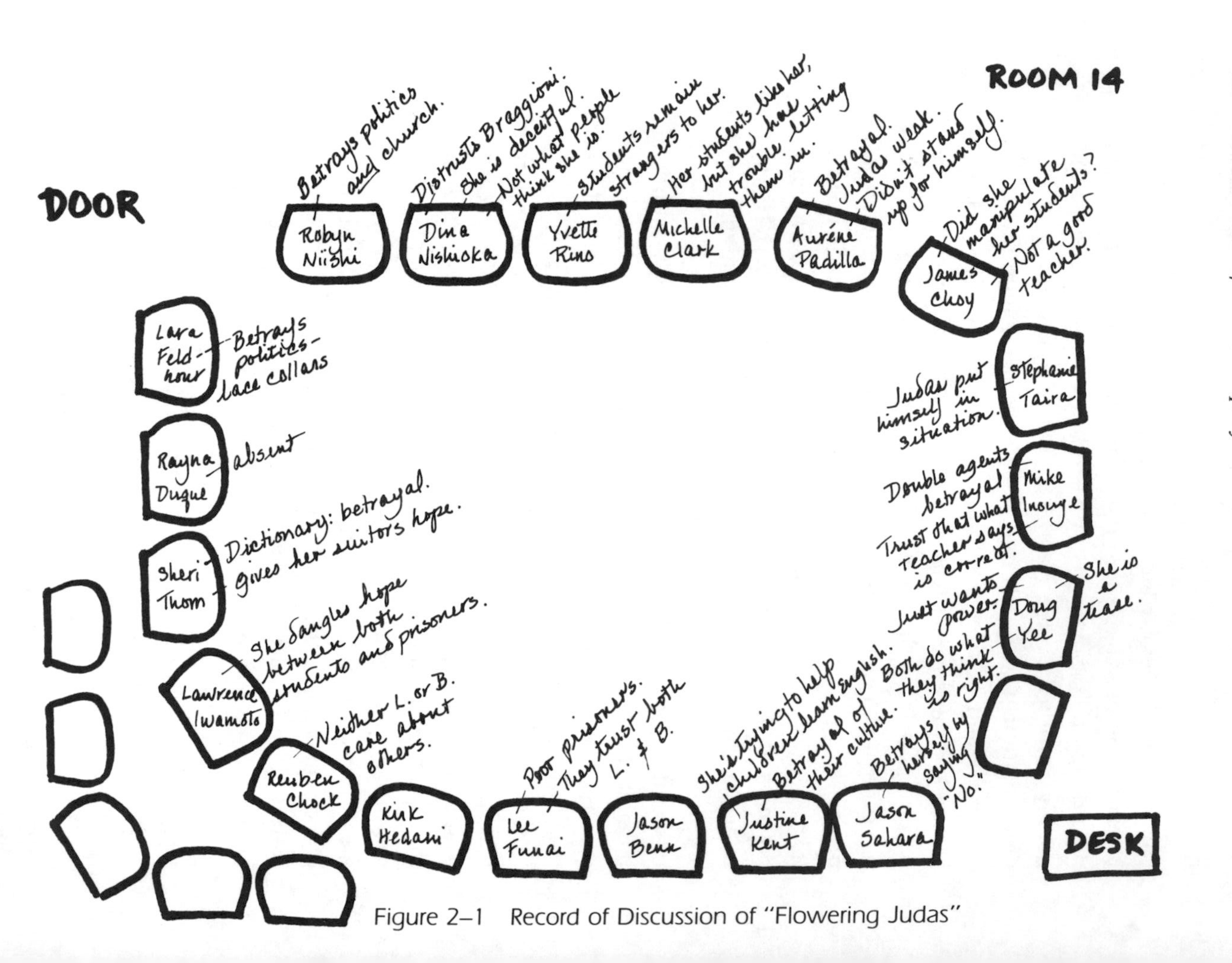

Figure 2–1 Record of Discussion of "Flowering Judas"

"What else did you notice?" "How did the rest of you try to resolve that issue?" "What else do we need to add here?" My opening questions are designed to be both specific and general. For example, although I focus student attention specifically on expectations gone awry as a point of entry, asking students to consider the implications of this theme, rather than asking them to define Crane's meaning, opens instead of narrows the topic.

Collaborative discussions are more successful when students have an opportunity to prepare individually before the discussion. I rely on similar preparation for the second and third days of discussion, using two assignments that help students come ready to contribute.

With *The Red Badge of Courage*, we begin with an exploration of character first because the class has prior experience with the concept and should be able to apply the analytical skills developed earlier. I have them begin in groups for peer support and feedback. Dividing the class into four groups, I give each responsibility for one character. This is how the exercise is presented:

THE RED BADGE OF COURAGE: CHARACTER DEVELOPMENT

Each group is responsible for exploring references to one of the following characters:

- Jim Conklin (the tall soldier, the spectral soldier)
- Wilson (the loud soldier)
- The Tattered Man (Chapters 8–10)
- The Cheery Man (Chapter 12)

For Homework:
List the words and phrases used to describe these characters. In what activities do they participate? How do they compare/contrast with one another? With Henry? What function(s) do they seem to serve in the novel as a whole? IMPORTANT: Please bring your written notes to class. You will not be able to participate in class discussion without them.

When students come to class the next day, they assemble in their groups, share their findings, and prepare a summary for the class as a whole. Often, I ask the groups to list key points on an overhead transparency, or to write a brief (one to two paragraph) summary of their observations to publish for the class. As the groups work, I circulate and check to see that everyone has done the assignment; students without notes are removed from the group and given another topic to prepare individually. Again, the message I wish to send is that doing the assignment is less work than **not** doing it. Students quickly learn that it is smarter to prepare for group discussion than to be stuck doing the same amount of work without support.

By the fourth day of the unit, I am assured that the group has a good literal understanding of the novel and is familiar with many of its details. I am ready to introduce them to a new concept: Naturalism. I begin by having students look up the word in a handbook of literary terms and bring a written definition to class. In class, we sort through the inevitable gobbledygook to arrive at two ideas central to understanding Naturalism: (1) humans are animals in the natural world; and (2) humans have neither control nor full understanding of the environmental forces and inner drives to which they respond (Holman 1972). Working in groups, students search the text for passages or incidents that they feel express that ontological view. Many are likely to cite Henry's encounter with the squirrel, for example, and his subsequent observation of a small animal catching a fish in the black bog water (chapter 7). Those students who remember their readings of Emerson will properly recognize Crane's ironic juxtaposition of two different worldviews. We finish the day's work by having groups share and explain their findings.

When working with a concept such as imagery or Naturalism, I often use the following progression: (1) discussion and modeling involving the entire class; (2) small group work with the same concept in new, but related, material; and (3) individual practice with, and both peer and teacher evaluation of, the same concept in new material. Having given students a supported sequence, I am then free to reuse the concept with new material, either as a group or individual activity (depending upon the complexity), throughout the course.

As an example, here are the experiences students have as they focus on patterns of imagery during the fifth and sixth days of our work with *The Red Badge of Courage*. They have already worked with imagery in an earlier poetry unit; now, they are ready to apply the concept to new content with group support. These are the directions:

THE RED BADGE OF COURAGE: PREPARATION FOR GROUP DISCUSSION ON IMAGERY

Each group is responsible for one of the following areas of exploration:

- Nature and reference to the natural landscape: What is the relationship of nature to events in the novel? How does Henry perceive nature? Are Henry's perceptions consistent with Crane's beliefs about nature? (Remember our work with the concept of Naturalism.)
- Hunger and thirst/eating and drinking: How are these feelings/activities described? When do they take place? Who participates? What patterns can you find?
- Animals and their behavior: What sorts of animals are referred to? How are they used? What animal(s) does Henry encounter directly? What are the effects/values of these encounters?

Directions:

1. Identify and list as many specific references as you can BEFORE you begin to draw conclusions. Divide the book among group members in order to cover the entire text thoroughly.
2. Come to class with your list and a written statement of your conclusions.
3. You will have time at the beginning of the hour to meet and prepare your analysis before presenting it to the entire class.

Typically, the group collaboration, the reports, and the ensuing discussions take almost two days and bring us to the final day of the unit. While we have not said all that we might about the text, students have ranged through it several times to collect material for class discussion, and we have used it to develop both the knowledge and skills necessary for critical inquiry. We know it well.

Our final day of discussion is reserved for various unresolved issues and questions that have arisen. In preparation for this discussion, a large sheet of manila paper labeled "Class Questions About *The Red Badge of Courage*" has been hung in a prominent place in the classroom; by the last day, it usually is quite full. (Early in the course, I plan activities specifically designed to help students generate questions to list here. They learn that, even if they see questions similar to theirs, they should enter their questions so that we don't miss any important nuances. Students quickly become familiar with the sheet and add their queries without prodding or monitoring.) We then categorize the questions and use them to guide our discussion.

Once again, a careful disorderliness is our method. We have issues to address, but the order in which we do so has emerged organically rather than having been determined by me. We have questions to be answered, but they are real questions, framed by real students about issues of real concern. As we complete our discussion, every member of the class can add an emerging command of the text's many patterns and details to his or her strong literal command of it.

At this point, rather than focus my evaluation on details of the text itself, I want to give students an individual experience dealing with patterns of imagery. In addition, I want to teach them how to include directly quoted material in their writing. These are the directions for the final assignment of the unit:

IMAGERY IN *THE RED BADGE OF COURAGE*

> In class, we discussed several patterns of imagery in this book: nature, hunger and thirst/eating and drinking, and animals. There are other patterns as well, including flags, light and dark, color, and smoke and haze. Choose one of these (or another that you have noticed) and repeat the process you went through to prepare for group discussion: search the text for references, list them, define some patterns, and draw some conclusions.
>
> Write a paper, which will be published for your classmates, in which you share your findings. Once you have determined your topic and collected material from the text, arrange a writer's conference with me. Drafts are due for peer evaluation on ———. Final papers are due on ———.

As students repeat the text search they experienced earlier, they reinforce and internalize patterns of returning to a literary text to see what it offers for comment. They are looking to see what emerges rather than seeking support for a preconceived thesis. Asking them to confer with me early in the writing gives me an opportunity to coach and assist them when such intervention is most productive: during the process of composition. Further, the assignment provides a chance to use peer response to help produce a formal, polished piece of writing. Finally, the writing has a real purpose and a real audience. Students are working to expand their classmates' understanding of a shared text. They are adding their voices to a real critical conversation.

Clearly, in a collaborative classroom, students' own experiences with texts must be central. Students learn to read by reading and by articulating their experiences and observations—to themselves, to their peers, to their teachers, to all members of the interpretive community. Answering the study questions provided by publishers is often a barren task because they are unrelated to the questions of the real community. Students recognize this intuitively and respond (perhaps appropriately) in mechanical, detached ways. Reading and writing need to be real. They need to have real value to students if they are to be taken seriously.

Teachers of literature need to know more than the historical background of a text, an author's biography, the critical controversies surrounding the text, and the conventional interpretations (if any) that prevail. Teachers also need to know how readers make meaning, how texts instruct readers on how to read and write them, and how readers and texts are the products of cultural contexts for reading and writing.[1] These epistemological issues form the basis from which to explore individual texts and the background and commentary in which they are embedded—their intertextuality and their contextuality.

Part of the teacher's job is to make students' experiences with texts transparent and available for analysis and discussion. By helping students examine their individual encounters with texts and then compare them among themselves, we help them develop some general principles of literary operation.

Another part of our job is to make literary context and intertextuality—the relationships among texts—accessible to students. New Criticism's overemphasis on texts as isolated things to be examined minutely paid little or no attention to authors or their expressed intentions, to the biographical, historical, and cultural contexts out of which texts emerge, or to the relationships between and among texts. Textual isolation diminishes our systems of inquiry to the point of sterility. Students deserve a fuller sense of the scope of the discipline.

We can help students formulate and pose questions about texts. We can teach them how to experience texts as fully as possible, to confront the gaps and indeterminacies that interest Reader–Response critics and take them as points of critical departure. Robert Scholes notes that, "Our job is *not* to intimidate students with our own superior textual production [but] to encourage their own textual practice" (1985, 24–25).

Teachers must be more knowledgeable than before. We must be able to do more than explicate texts. We must recognize how we compose meanings and make our strategies available to students. We must know how our readings emerge and teach students how such information can be accessible to them as well.

Finally, as we teach literary composing—reading and writing—we have to be particularly sensitive to the nature of our teaching. Is our focus properly on product or process? On a combination of the two? At which points in our interactions with students, their purposes and needs as readers or writers, and our purposes and needs as teachers must our emphasis shift? The importance of these questions cannot be underestimated. Many of us unwittingly keep students dependent on us, rather than teaching them how to operate independently.[2]

Our former classroom model inevitably leads students to produce cold mashed potatoes. When students are limited to writing thesis-centered argument papers for an abstract audience, they invariably choose safe, simple content (Emig 1983, 66) that they can shape easily into proper academic form. Students remain uninvolved. They learn to view writing in school as an exercise, something to be done for agendas with which they are not personally connected. Our former model produces students who do not learn the heuristic power of writing and cannot tap that power, either for self-discovery or for discovery of the world outside the self. More unhappily, it produces students who feel no connection to a community mutually involved in using language for productive ends. When classroom tasks are artificial and stilted, when they lack meaning for the student, they are doomed to fail as useful educational activities.

Given the options, we have no choice but to reenvision what we are attempting in our classrooms. We have no choice but to embrace both critical process and critical product in our pedagogy. We have no choice but to learn to see ourselves as practitioners enabling critical conversations.

TEACHING CONNECTION AND PERCEPTION

INTRODUCTION

Our desire to help students develop a lifetime appreciation for good literature is a controlling force behind what we literature teachers do. We want students to love the novels and plays and poems that we love. We want them to nod appreciatively at turns of phrase or poetic rhythms that please our ears. We want them to chuckle with us at the human condition and to weep where our tears have stained pages. We want them to enjoy the same pleasures—emotional, critical, and aesthetic—that we do when we read.

It's not so easy. Students come to our classes with a number of suspicions and erroneous assumptions about the nature of interactions between texts and readers. They believe literature is full of hidden meanings that they will be incapable of ferreting out, and they feel teachers have secret knowledge that enables successful interpretation. They suspect that nicer teachers would make life happier by revealing meanings, instead of making students thrash around in a slough of poetic despond, trying to make sense of a literary mire.

Students believe that each poem or novel or story or play has one true meaning that can be expressed aphoristically in phrases such as "honesty is the best policy" (for *The Scarlet Letter*, perhaps) or "war is hell" (for *The Red Badge of Courage*). Finding this true meaning is a guessing game with obscure rules, for which students never have all the necessary information. Literary encounters become clever traps that affirm students' feelings of ignorance and failure as readers.

This reductionist view of the literary encounter as the search for Truth limits students' range of experiences with texts and, ironically enough, leads to the fulfillment of their pessimistic expectations. Not only do they get no pleasure from literary experiences, they never manage to understand the nature of those experiences very well. They never feel that they are, or can become, competent, participating members in the club of critical inquiry to which their teachers so comfortably belong.

If we are going to help students join our club, we must change their old beliefs and habits. We must teach them to accept variant readings of the same text. We must show them that critical inquiry requires both personal connection and critical distancing and that shortchanging one limits the potential of the other. They must learn that inquiry is a process that requires engagement and re-engagement with both text and critical conversation.

Peter Elbow reminds us that teaching means affecting the way that a student "files his data, processes his information, or makes his inferences" (1986, 11). Elbow is not talking about conveying information but about teaching methodology—teaching process. Elbow means that we needn't be concerned so much with particular data as with students' abilities to encode and use data productively. Instruction should center on efforts to develop students into sophisticated practitioners in our field. We need to teach students how to change the lens through which they view texts. We need to teach them to see as readers, see as writers, and see as collaborative talkers in their literature classrooms.

In other words, if we want students to succeed in their encounters with literary texts, we need to shift our (and their) attention from the content of particular works to the processes of reading and responding to them in general. First, we need to attend to students' responses to understand how they are processing information and making literary inferences. And we need to teach them to trust and pay attention to those responses. Many students deny the value of their experiences with texts, dismissing them prematurely.

Teachers need instruments that analyze student needs appropriately. If we ask students to work well above their levels of competence, they fail to comprehend. They sublimate the personal frustration (engendered by failure) by responding hostilely to the text that represents the failure. Further, when we focus on text content by asking students to respond, for example, to a series of short-answer questions, we deflect attention from larger textual elements and may actually interfere with students' abilities to approach thematic issues. Our interference ultimately sabotages our attempts to evaluate student performance reliably.

Critical discourse—writing and talking within a community of inquirers—provides a useful and reliable tool that can be used repeatedly in various forms. Student language about texts can be used to make their processes of composing meaning transparent. Once the processes are transparent, they become available for discussion. Students can see what they do and what they might do. They can revise, or add to, composing strategies. Student language also provides a window on the meanings composed by student and text. Conversation awards communal validity to interpretations or suggests a need for revision. Seeing both what and how students compose in response to texts, we can evaluate their levels of comfortable engagement and guide them to more complex modes of engagement.

Perhaps our first task is to teach students to encounter literature flexibly. However, convincing students that texts are not closed, determinate receptacles of meaning is a difficult task. Printed pages bound within covers suggest permanence. For students, learning that understanding a text is a subjective activity—dependent upon what a reader knows prior to reading, what the text offers, and the context (for both reader and text) in which the reading is done—requires them to reconceptualize what reading means. That reconceptualization helps students become receptive to the subjective nature of textual experiences.

Learning to discriminate between the solidity of the visible surface structure and the fluctuating, invisible text world the pages potentially contain requires practice. Students get such practice by sharing their responses to texts. Writing and talking about texts is part of an ongoing human discussion—what Kenneth Bruffee has called "the conversation of mankind" (1984). Within the contexts of these discussions, students will discover that meanings are changing relationships, heavily dependent on context and point of view. Text worlds differ. Readers bring different background information to a text; they notice things others miss; they focus attention differently.

Encouraging such discoveries and discussing them empowers students in their encounters with texts because it teaches them that they are free to be tentative, speculative, and exploratory. Encouraging a sense of discovery releases students from the fear of being wrong and allows them to acknowledge their personal responses to texts. This shift is crucial. As students talk and listen to one another, they test their experiences against the observations of others. Doing so, they distance themselves from both text and experience and take the next step in critical inquiry.

The next three chapters discuss means to enable personal connection. They provide strategies for exploratory, tentative, speculative writing about literature. Each is designed to help students observe both texts and their own patterns of response to those texts.

The dialogue journal discussed in chapter 3 provides a strategy to help students take the first important steps in critical inquiry. First, they look carefully at what they notice in a text, then they respond personally to those noticings. Using the process log described in chapter 4 uncovers the strategies students bring to the reading of a particular text in order to help them refine and extend the range of techniques available to them. The reading response in chapter 5 provides a free-form mode of response and comment and enables students to discover and explore (at greater length) the issues and questions a text raises for them.

These response modes do not have to be taught in the order presented here. My arrangement simply reflects a logical (but not necessarily pedagogical) progression from a form that has the student look most closely at the text to one in which they write from a more distanced position. Nor should teachers ask students to use every form to respond to every text. The value of having three modes of response from which to choose is pedagogical. The particular way in which students engage with a text depends upon the text's complexity, the literary sophistication of the students relative to the text, and the objectives of the teacher and student.

Clearly, each chapter is underpinned by a belief that process needs to occupy a central position in our classrooms. Learning is more than the acquisition of skills. Learning includes knowing strategies of response and their appropriate applications; it means having general principles of categorization and operation that can serve in multiple situations. Learning itself is an ongoing process. We predict, assimilate, and order; we reevaluate and revise; we continually expand and redefine the schema by which we code our experience. Keeping this in mind clarifies the nature of our enterprise. Teaching is a matter of helping students learn how to think, how to acquire knowledge. Good teaching combines the acquisition of information with the acquisition of learning processes. Our intention is to help students become skilled in the processes of getting knowledge from literary texts and to help them gain confidence in their abilities as readers/composers of those texts.

Writing and reading are both processes of composing meaning, of connecting knowledge, of imposing order on chaotic potentiality. They are fundamentally similar activities, and writing is a powerful tool to help students understand the texts they read while they understand their processes responding to those texts. The advantages of bringing writing to the foreground of our literature classes are apparent. Not only do students acquire a useful and accessible means of practicing composing as readers, but they learn critical thinking through writing. No longer simply utilitarian, writing, as part of the process of genuine inquiry and the exercise of reasonable judgment, becomes an epistemological occasion in the fullest sense.

Readers/writers/talkers—as we ask students to shift lenses, the distinctions between the three blur and eventually collapse. With that collapse comes the destruction of earlier paradigms of reading and literary criticism. Students become free to emerge into the mature selfhood of thoughtful inquiry. As they move from reading to writing to talking, they become capable of sharing literary delights with us. They attain membership in our literary club.

3 Writing Next to Texts: Dialogue Journals

Double-entry notebooks, dialectical notebooks, or dialogue journals—the idea behind each is identical. Each allows students to record quotations, observations, lists, and images from their reading and then return to those entries for reflection and comment. Each provides a useful way for students to converse with themselves about both the what and the how of their reading. Each is a pedagogical tool permitting deliberate, strategic intervention in students' textual experiences.

In dialogue journals (as I call them), students use the left-hand pages of a notebook for quotations, jottings, or summaries. I ask them to label this, "What the Book Says." Later, they respond to, or comment on, this material with questions, sentences, and paragraphs on the appropriate facing pages. They label these pages, "What I Say." The idea is for the notebook to mimic the dialectic of content and comment, or text and metatext, that is reflective of students' composing processes as readers and writers. The back-and-forth movements between the observation and gathering of data for critical inquiry and the interpretation that takes place as the material is ordered and shaped (composed) become transparent to the composer. Students see both their immersion into a text as they record and their distancing from a text as they evaluate.[1] Such writing becomes, of course, the "commentation and exposition . . . by means of written words" that T. S. Eliot defines as criticism (1932, 13).

Let us see how a dialogue journal might work for a student. The left-hand pages enable a recording of those bits of a text that the student deems to be significant or interesting. Here is a page from a student's dialogue journal for *Rosencrantz and Guildenstern Are Dead*:

G:	There is an art to the building up of suspense.
R:	Heads (12).
G:	Is *that* what you imagine? Is that it? No *fear?*
R:	Fear?
G:	*Fear!* The crack that might flood your brain with light!
R:	Heads . . . (15).
G:	You don't get my meaning. What is the first thing after all the things you've forgotten?
R:	Oh I see. (Pause). I've forgotten the question (16).
R:	Another curious scientific phenomenon is the fact that the fingernails grow after death, as does the beard.
G:	What?
R:	Beard!
G:	But you're not dead (18).
Player:	It costs little to watch, and little more if you happen to get caught up in the action, if that's your taste and times being what they are.
R:	What are they?
Player:	Indifferent.
R:	Bad?
Player:	Wicked. Now what precisely is your pleasure? (23)
Player:	They're hardly divisible, sir—well, I can do your blood and love without the rhetoric, and I can do your blood and rhetoric without the love, and I can do your all three concurrent or consecutive, but I can't do your love and rhetoric without the blood. Blood's compulsory—they're all blood, you see (33).[2]

This student was selective in her entries. Often a page or two went by before she found a passage that she chose to record. Sometimes, she included the entire interchange between characters, sometimes only a single speech. But dialogue journals vary considerably in their form.

Another student in the same class developed a much more fragmentary method of recording passages as displayed by this segment of her journal from the first chapter of *A Portrait of the Artist*:

> "What's your father?" "A gentleman."
> "Is he a magistrate?" (9).
>
> "And his father told him . . . never to peach on a fellow" (9).
>
> It was like something in a book. . . . They were like poetry (10).
>
> tunnel sound (13).
>
> "He still tried to think what was the right answer" (15).
>
> maroon and green (15).
>
> Stephen Dedalus—class of elements— . . . The Universe (15).
>
> "Canker is a disease of plants/cancer one of animals" (21).
>
> "Parnell! Parnell! He is dead!" (Dante not bowing) (27).

Clearly, the form of this dialogue journal is highly idiosyncratic. Even a reader familiar with Joyce's work might have trouble making much sense out of this collection of phrases. That's fine; if the material makes sense to the student, it is filling its functions. Teachers must learn to read such private recordings for what they can learn about students' interactions with a text rather than for specific content.

Indeed, when students are learning to do dialogue journals, we need to remind them not to be terribly judgmental in their selection of items to record; they should simply include passages that resonate, even if they are uncertain why they do so. Furthermore, we need to help students discover a form with which they are comfortable. Some will benefit from including extended passages, while others do well working with more abbreviated selections. It may, in fact, be wise to teach the use of the ellipsis so students can shorten lengthy quotations. Finally, while direct quotations are probably the most useful, students might also wish to jot down details of plot, character, or setting that strike them.

As we begin class discussion, students share with their classmates what they have noticed, focusing first on similarities in observation. The aim is to build confidence; students learn that what they notice is "right" because it coincides with what stands out for many others. Next, we look at those things included by fewer people. I try to get students to articulate why they recorded certain details and to identify precisely what generated a particular question. Acceptance of differing student offerings again works to build confidence.

Once we have discussed this aspect of the journals thoroughly, I startle students by asking, "If each of you has a different reporting of what you noticed, and some people even have bits or questions here that no one else has, whose dialogue journal is right?" It doesn't take long for even the most insecure to realize that, as long as the job has been done thoroughly, it is right, even though it may be different.

After students have the confidence of that realization, they are ready to take the next critical step. The left-hand pages of dialogue journals help students reach a personally coherent and satisfying reading of a text's meanings and complexities. Having completed a reading, the next critical step is to distance themselves sufficiently from the text to recognize its significances. It is not enough for students to know that Hester Prynne meets Arthur Dimmesdale in the forest; critical readers must also be sensitive to the issues raised by that meeting in the context of the work as a whole. In the same way, students reading *Great Expectations* must not only recognize Miss Havisham's encapsulation in a world of loveless moral and physical decay but seek the implications of that decay throughout the novel.

The right-hand pages of the dialogue journal lead students to understanding such implications. Here is the selection cited earlier from the first dialogue journal on *Rosencrantz and Guildenstern* with the relevant commentary from the right-hand pages.

<table>
<tr><td>G:
R:</td><td>There is an art to the building up of suspense.
Heads (12).</td><td>The two (G & R) are such simpletons. This is a typical conversation, with one trying to talk philosophy or science and the other simply irrational or dumb, not understanding.</td></tr>
<tr><td>G:
R:
G:
R:</td><td>Is *that* what you imagine? Is that it? No *fear?*
Fear?
Fear! The crack that might flood your brain with light!
Heads . . . (15).</td><td>There's a whole business of fear and being afraid. So what? They don't seem to take fear very seriously (their coin toss game continues).</td></tr>
<tr><td>G:
R:</td><td>You don't get my meaning. What is the first thing after all the things you've forgotten?
Oh I see. (Pause). I've forgotten the question (16).</td><td>Another typical & stupid conversation. They confuse the meaning of everything each other says. (They are getting to be like Oliver and Hardy!!)</td></tr>
<tr><td>R:
G:
R:
G:</td><td>Another curious scientific phenomenon is the fact that the fingernails grow after death, as does the beard.
What?
Beard!
But you're not dead (18).</td><td>More ridiculous, scientific junk.</td></tr>
<tr><td>Player:
R:
Player:
R:
Player:</td><td>It costs little to watch, and little more if you happen to get caught up in the action, if that's your taste and times being what they are.
What are they?
Indifferent.
Bad?
Wicked. Now what precisely is your pleasure? (23)</td><td>The preciseness of the words of the Player really stand out because R & G are so dumb.</td></tr>
<tr><td>Player:</td><td>They're hardly divisible, sir—well, I can do your blood and love without the rhetoric, and I can do your</td><td>Well, of course, the Player does use rhetoric also. But his rhetoric makes sense.</td></tr>
</table>

> blood and rhetoric without the love, and I can do your all three concurrent or consecutive, but I can't do your love and rhetoric without the blood. Blood's compulsory—they're all blood, you see (33).

The dialogue journal allowed this student to express her irritation as she reacted scornfully to the absurdity of the exchanges between Rosencrantz and Guildenstern. She then began to recognize the pattern of absurdity ("another typical & stupid conversation"). She also began to define and accept the comic nature of the exchanges between Rosencrantz and Guildenstern, noting, "They are getting to be like Oliver and Hardy!!"

Furthermore, this reader was poised on the edge of identifying the pattern of failed communication that is thematically central to the play. She saw Rosencrantz and Guildenstern as "not understanding" and asserted, "They confuse the meaning of everything each other says." She compared their language with the "preciseness of the words of the Player" and suggested that, while the Player used rhetoric, "his rhetoric makes sense." By the time she joined the class discussion, this student had many useful observations to share.

In a dialogue journal, students focus attention both on the content of a text and on their observation of that content. They explore what they use to compose literary texts, to make meaning from words on a page. They begin to see the dialogue between text and receiver. Their analysis of that dialogue centers on the reading-as-composing processes as much as it does on the meanings offered them by the text. To that end, students experiment with various, self-selected ways of commenting on their observations. Then, once they have developed their own modes of response, they are ready to be introduced to variations and explore their composing processes more consciously.

Asking students to connect a literary text to their personal lives is a common teaching strategy that is important on several levels. Such connections provide students with opportunities to validate personal responses; they also serve to collapse surface differences of time, location, race, class, and sex and to suggest generalizations about universal aspects of the human experience. Often, the personal response is what ultimately ushers a reader into a particularly complex work. The first chapter of *Ulysses,* for example, is made accessible because of what we may know about typical relationships within groups of young men, between mothers and their sons, and within a nation that is politically dominated by another.

Here is part of another dialogue journal, this one devoted to John Howard Griffin's *Black Like Me* (1976). Its style is quite different, from the previous one presented, revealing a different critical persona and an intentional focus on making personal connections.

"It was unlike anything I had imagined. I became two men, the observing one and the one who panicked, who felt Negroid even into the depths of his entrails. I felt the beginnings of great loneliness, not because I was a Negro, but because the man I had been, I knew, was hidden in the flesh of another. I had tampered with the mystery of existence and I had lost the sense of my own being" (16).	This is Griffin's first experience as a Negro. The change for him seemed traumatic but he knew he had to adjust to it. It must have been fright ening because it was like losing all of his securities and self confidence because he did not really know who the self he was as a Negro. It was an identity he could not recognize and had to learn how to build it up properly.
"Here hips drew the eye and flirted with the eye and caused the eye to lust or laugh. It was better to look at hips than at the ghetto" (22).	I like the use of repetitive words. Also it describes Griffin's (one of his) opinions about the ghetto and how he's trying to adjust. Trying to be one of them. He's scoping this area out and is still figuring out his identity.

While this dialogue journal is critical ("I like the use of repetitive words") and interpretive ("The change for him seemed traumatic"), the language suggests a writer who is trying to define and understand the nature of another's experience. The student sympathizes, "It must have been frightening," and recognizes Griffin's attempt to connect in his new community as he is "trying to be one of them." Even the writer's reversion to adolescent slang ("he's scoping this area out") suggests a linguistic attempt to bridge experiential gaps and find a common human thread in Griffin's need to keep "figuring out his identity." The dialogue journal gives proper legitimacy to the personal responses we all make in initial encounters with texts, while highlighting the active role of readers as composers of texts. In the process, it lessens students' inclination to await passively the conveyance of Truth from text or teacher.

A second strategy borrows from Reader–Response theory, most especially from Walker Gibson's notion of the "mock reader" (1983, 1–6) and Gerald Prince's vision of the "narratee" (1980, 7–25). Here, students choose a quotation that has particular resonance and write a description—physical, social, and psychological—of the kind of reader the language of the passage creates and assumes. Students learn to ask, "Who, exactly, is the narrator speaking to?" This activity is particularly useful prior to a class discussion exploring the roles that different texts create for their readers and how we, as readers, assume those roles for the duration of a text.[3] It is also useful when dealing with a text such as *The Sound and the Fury* or *Bleak House,* which uses multiple narrators.

Such discussions provide fruitful entry into class considerations of genre as well. The lyric poem, for example, suggests an intimate and less judgmental relationship between narrator and reader than the ironic distance typical of many novels. When students understand how an author positions readers in reference to a text, they become conscious of conventions of response. They also recognize the critical implications imbedded in the position a reader assumes relative to a particular text.

Two other comment modes depend on the conscious use of a negative. In one, students are asked to write about what they *didn't* notice or record in the text. They look at what is missing, what things an author might have made explicit but chose not to. Then, they speculate as to why particular choices were made.

Ulysses again provides a convenient illustration because of the myriad textual interpolations it demands of readers. In chapter 1, for example, when an old milk woman arrives at the tower where Stephen and his friends are living, a brief paragraph begins, "Stephen listened in scornful silence" (1986, 12, 1.418). In that paragraph, Joyce gives us Stephen's reflections on a conversation among Stephen's two roommates and the woman but not a record of the conversation that forms the background for those reflections, even though it is clearly an important part of Stephen's experience. Stephen's question to the woman, "Did you understand what he said?" and the following dialogue allow us to intuit that Haines (one of the young men) has spoken in Gaelic. While Stephen's question provides implicit evidence of the detail, the reader must make the detail explicit to understand central implications of the scene. Students looking at similar scenes learn to fill in gaps in a narrative and to speculate on the effects of those gaps.

Another negative activity is based on what Elbow calls "a cognitive dissonance model" (1986, 95). Students write oppositions to several quotations that they included among their entries. That is, they reverse the meanings of the original however they can. They do this whether they believe their oppositions or not. Simply seeing the original juxtaposed to its antithesis increases the number of ways in which they think about it.

Another comment mode acquaints students with the rich layers of meaning embodied in words. They pick a single word from one of their chosen quotations and, saying it aloud several times, savoring its sound, its physicality in the mouth, write a comment exploring its feelings. They then find the word in a good dictionary, copy out its multiple meanings, and comment again. Students typically discover that a word's evocations are the result of more than felt sense; learning this, they acquire an important critical tool.

Two other comment modes also help increase student awareness of their interactions with texts. Taking several pages of initial journal entries, students group and classify as many as possible. They experiment with different categories: emotions, places, kinds of people, words beginning with vowels, things my sister would hate, or whatever. After some initial assistance, we can trust student imagination to invent new ways of categorizing collected material. Some groupings provide a more useful basis for critical inquiry than others, but the activity encourages an imaginative range of ways to classify patterns in literary material, and students become receptive to the potency of nontraditional groupings. Useful critical observation often begins with the valuable ability to form unlikely connections.

Another activity has students write questions next to as many entries as possible. Questions might ask why a passage is phrased as it is or how a passage is appropriate to the work as a whole. Students might wonder what another reader (real or fictional) would find important or interesting in the passage. Here are sample questioning entries generated by the opening pages of *Great Expectations* (1973):

"memorable, raw afternoon towards evening" (9).	What's a "raw" afternoon?
"At such a time I found out for certain that this place overgrown with nettles was the churchyard; and that Philip Pirrip, late of this Parish, and Also Georgiana wife of the same, were dead and buried . . . " (10).	What brought on such a sudden enlightenment concerning his parents? He still seems to think that "Philip Pirrip, late of this Parish," is his father's full name, and that "Also Georgiana" is his mother's name. Is this ignorance being compared to his later intellectual advancement?
"The marshes were just long black horizontal lines when I stopped to look after him . . . dense black lines intermixed (13).	Dark images dominant in the background scenery. Why did he think of horizontal lines? Why not strips or ribbons or something like that? These dark images might represent the convict and his evils that engulf Pip or they may be foreshadowing Pip's future being like "dense black lines intermixed."

The act of questioning is central to critical inquiry. Janice Lauer claims such inquiry begins with "dissonance and well-articulated unknowns" (1982, 91). Yet dissonance terrifies most students. They yearn for certainty. Instead of struggling to articulate their unknowns, they fear their questions, misreading them as signs of stupidity or ignorance rather than as directional guides for critical thinking. When a teacher asks, "Are there any questions?" the silence that follows is not as much a signal of the absence of dissonance as it is a sign of students' reluctance to reveal uncertainty.

Sharing questions in class shows students the multiple possibilities of inquiry into texts. As a group, they experience the multiplicity of meaning inherent in all discourse. Questions raised by classmates lead to discussions that make it impossible to believe texts have single meanings. If dialogue journals served no pedagogical function but to reveal this truth, they would still be invaluable tools for teaching critical inquiry. Their very tentativeness causes students quickly to abandon their belief in (and fruitless search for) single Truths in texts.

The shape of the critical question limits or enhances critical response. Comprehension is fundamentally dependent on the questions readers ask (or might productively ask) of a text. Indeed, literary theorists can be usefully classified by the focus of their questions: on author (Biographical and Psychoanalytic critics), on text (New critics and Structuralists), on reader (Reader–Response critics), or on context (Historists, Marxist critics, Phenomenologists, Feminists). Students and teachers need not embrace any single critical doctrine. All legitimate questions are available in our classrooms.

A three-step sequence using dialogue journals provides an especially useful way to help students prepare for a critical paper on a lengthy text, such as a novel. In the first stage, the journal is completed, as usual, while students are reading; they follow the standard procedure of collecting quotations, jottings, and summaries on one page and writing periodic responses on the facing page.

When they have finished reading and commenting, they reread their entire dialogue with the work, generating as many questions as they can. Listing all their questions on one side of a new page, they use the facing page to group and respond to their questions. Their objective is to define areas of inquiry and discover questions worthy of extended critical exploration. After group discussion of the questions (with potential revision), students are ready to identify questions for their personal inquiry.

Having determined an area of inquiry, students return to the text to search for quotations. In their dialogue journals, they list everything that seems pertinent to their exploration. After mining the text for raw material, the facing pages of their journals await, ready for the observations and responses they compose, ready to generate the draftings of their final papers. By now, students are ready to use the commentary pages eclectically, drawing from a wide repertoire of response modes. Their responses become self-rhythmed and various. They come to their writing with a keen sense of what they perceive in the text, how they feel about what they see, and the critical associations that inform and follow from their perceptions.

Here is the first part of a dialogue journal written by a young man preparing to write a paper about Addie in *As I Lay Dying*:

"I could just remember how my father used to say that the reason for living was to get ready to stay dead for a long time" (155).	I picture Addie's father as a practical man that did not dwell on many intangible objects like afterlife but lived for the present.
" 'They turned out real nice!' I say. 'But not like the cakes Addie used to bake' " (7).	Here I know Addie bakes well.
". . . I had Cash, I knew living was terrible and that this was the answer for it" (151). "When he was born I knew that motherhood was invented by someone who . . ." (157).	This sentence shocked and puzzled me. Obviously it seems as though she did not want Cash. I wasn't certain. I feel bad knowing Cash did all he could for Addie and originally he had been an unwanted child.
"I knew fear was invented by someone that . . ." (157).	Addie is very critical about life and her problems make her seem very pessimistic.
"My revenge would be that he would never know I was taking revenge" (159).	I'm not sure what the revenge is for and who it is against. Perhaps it is against Anse. She had an affair and Anse didn't.

This student uses his commentary to generate hypotheses (Addie's father lives for the present, Addie is taking revenge against Anse), to identify and personalize his own knowledge ("I know Addie bakes well"), to explore his personal response to Addie (her attitudes puzzle and shock him), and to generate some generalizations about Addie's views of the world (she is pessimistic).

When students separate fragments of text from the imposing whole, and record them in their own handwriting, the original words are demystified and made accessible to apprentice critics. Students grow to feel comfortable articulating the connections, the meanings, they have found in the text. Unvoiced, such meanings are less available for evaluation and revision; once recorded in a dialogue journal, however, they can be returned to, rethought, and revalidated. In the following sample dialogue journal, a student made discoveries about Dewey Dell in *As I Lay Dying* that gave her material she was able to use in her final paper.

"We picked on down the row, . . . the secret shade . . . my sack and Lafe's sack . . . our eyes would drown together touching . . . I could not help it" (23–24).	Dewey shows that she can't help it if Lafe gets to sleep with her. After all, what if her sack is filled? She has no control over the situation. What a sincere floozy. She's young, naive and much like Anse Bundren.
"And he doesn't even know it. . . . It lies dead and warm upon me . . . hot blind earth" (58).	Dewey, alone and confused (as any young country motherless woman would be), doesn't know what to do. She doesn't know how to feel. She is experiencing a time of merged death and birth.

The last sentence of each comment records the generation of an insight into the text that the student did not have before she began to explore the quoted passage in her own language.

The dialogue journal is a useful way to teach critical inquiry because it demands the primary critical stance: arrested attention. Students must look . . . and look again. The dialogue journal teaches students the same lessons of close and repeated attention that Agassiz taught with his fish (Shaler 1967). They learn firsthand the usefulness of Northrop Frye's observation that "the fundamental critical act . . . is the act of recognition" (1970, 68).

Arrested attention also leads students to acquire what Eliot called "a very highly developed sense of fact" (1932, 19). Lists of textual details generate questions, patterns, and comment. The dialogue between the textual fact and critical interpretation is visually available on the pages of the dialogue journals. The entire process of this dialogue forces students to practice comparison and analysis—fundamental critical tools.

While they look, students gain consciousness of themselves as critical inquirers. They distance themselves from their engagement with texts. They learn how they abstract. The distance enabled by dialogue journals makes explicit connections between text and prior knowledge. As a result, students prepare to move smoothly from the concrete to the abstract, from personal response to expository essay. As critics, they learn to recognize what they know and its values.

Furthermore, the dialogue journal stresses the rich potential of possible responses. Responding in varying ways teaches students the value of keeping options open and tolerating ambiguity. Giving up an unproductive search for textual certainty, students are ready to learn the generative power of chaos.

Looking, distancing, manipulating—that is what the dialogue journal enables. Not only does it position students close to the text, it enables them to observe and control their movements as readers.

4 Writing Through Texts: Process Logs

A log is a series of written entries recording progress over a period of time. Process logs enable students to articulate their progress as they identify the analytical strategies that they use with particular texts. When process logs are used with texts that are difficult for students to enter (poetry, or the opening passages of Joyce's *A Portrait of the Artist,* or Benjy's section in Faulkner's *The Sound and the Fury,* for example), they serve to teach students new techniques for making meaning. Articulating their composing processes as they encounter texts, students share with classmates the strategies of evolving comprehension. Hearing how others entered a work, they discover possible strategies that they have not applied. Like dialogue journals, the process logs help students move from an initial, personal engagement with a text to the less personal but more self-aware distance required for skilled critical abstraction.

Here are sample directions for a process log about a poem:

PROCESS LOG

We will be discussing this poem in class shortly. Please follow these directions for reading and thinking about the poem.

1. Read the poem through once, slowly. Do not make any marks or notes on this reading; simply get an overall understanding of the subject of the poem and author's attitude. In one or two sentences, write a statement of what you think the SUBJECT of the poem is and briefly state what the narrator seems to be saying about the subject.

2. Read the poem a second time, marking the text and making marginal notes. Reread what you wrote in #1. Write a revised statement if you wish. If not, write "okay."

3. Write a process log of your reading, in which you describe as fully as possible the PROCESS of your reading. The following questions may guide your thinking about that process:

- What did you understand, think, feel after your first reading?
- What questions did you have?
- What words/phrases were confusing?
- What words/phrases helped your understanding?
- What words/phrases seemed to have particular importance? Can you tell why?
- As you read the poem a second time, marking it, what insights did you have?
- What areas are still confusing to you?
- What feelings does the poem evoke for you?
- What meanings do you feel the poem is expressing?

Use freewriting (start writing and keep writing) for your process log. Do not be concerned if you have questions and uncertainties; simply try to identify them as specifically as you can. You are trying to describe HOW you read and understood as well as WHAT you read and understood.

Here is an example of a student process log written in response to Elizabeth Bishop's poem, "Brazil, January 1, 1502":

Hmmm...what is this poem talking about? Is the second stanza the entire big part and the lizard part or just the big part? There doesn't seem to be a rhyme scheme or a set meter. It's sort of strange that each stanza (I guess except in the lizard one if it's not a part of stanza 2) has an odd number of lines.

The influence of Brazil is evident in stanza 1 as the flora described obviously can only exist in a January of a tropical country. The images in stanza 1 seem fresh and pleasant. However, the fact of "every square inch filling with foliage" seems overbearing. There's fresh, airy plants, but there are so many that it seems heavy and overbearing.

In stanza 2A (that's the big part) there seems to be an element of hiding. The birds perch in profile, therefore hiding half of their faces,

> "each showing only half his . . . breast." Then, all of a sudden (this scared me the first time) there's "Sin" (with a capital "S") in the foreground. Then there's all the things about moss and vines attacking rocks.
>
> In stanza 2B I don't understand how the lizards in heat come about. Maybe they symbolize humans and the way they act out of desire and pleasure rather than out of intelligence (leading to "Sin"?)
>
> The third stanza obviously criticizes those Christians who act holy and innocent but actually are not. What is the point of this poem? Maybe the fact that man tends to disguise his desires but is actually sinful. But then, why would "Sin" be in the foreground? Is it because the narrator believes that sin dominates society?

The tone of the log is informal. The writer was talking to herself on paper, probing the poem for coherence, trying to find clues in its structure and form. This student made several useful observations (the overabundance of foliage, the hidden nature of the birds in profile, the frightening way in which sin is brought to the foreground). While there were no firm answers, we can observe emerging understanding.

Writing a process log helps understanding emerge because the directions lead students through several important phases of critical inquiry. The first reading of the poem provides an orientation. The reader develops an overall feel for the text and becomes sensitive to problems it presents. Student logs written in response to William Cullen Bryant's "Thanatopsis" reveal differing processes of orientation. One student wrote:

> The first thing I got was that the poem was about Nature's power. The poet refers to this by using "Nature" with a capital "N." I wasn't sure exactly what this Nature was exactly powerful over. It wasn't clear (in the first reading).

For this student, a first reading led to a notion of the poem's general subject while generating a central question for examination during the next reading. The explicit articulation of the question oriented the reader toward a way to find meanings in the text.

Another student expressed similar confusion after a first reading:

> I didn't know what Bryant was talking about. Actually I got the basic subjects: Nature, Men, and the Earth, but I missed the most important theme, death! At the end of the poem I was so lost, that I even wondered . . . who is he talking about dying at the end: Just man, or anything in general?

This reader also found useful orientation in the articulation of the specific problems the text poses and even developed an awareness of the value of articulation. The next paragraph of the same log reads:

> I found everything much easier to understand because when I read it the second time, I already knew what questions I was trying to answer. I could then look for the answer and make sense of the surrounding words and lines by fitting everything together.

The orientation developed during the first reading helped this reader approach a second encounter with the text with a sense of purpose. That sense of purpose provided productive direction.

For another student, the poem's form presented initial difficulty:

> The first few lines seemed unintelligible when read to conform to a rhythm or rhyme pattern. Upon starting over, I found that it is easier to understand if the poem is read as if it were prose, that is as if there were periods and proper capitals.

Defining the location of the difficulty allowed this student to re-orient reading strategies productively.

Another phase of inquiry is the development of a hypothesis. Hypothesis generating typically comes as the confirmation of an orientation. Orientation generates questions ("What is this about?" "How should I read?"); the hypothesis provides tentative answers to these questions. By attempting to articulate a statement of the poem's overall subject, students come to grips in a general way with the relationships (explicit or perhaps still implicit) in the text. This hypothesis then serves as a search model for the next reading of the poem. One process log provides a clear window on the moment such a hypothesis developed:

> A lot of things didn't make sense until I neared the middle of [the poem] and understood that the author was trying to reassure the reader that death was not to be feared.

Having identified a central point of the poem, the reader then moved to the next critical steps.

An aspect of critical inquiry is definition. The reader seeks clarification of terms and concepts (words and phrases that need further analysis perhaps). An excerpt from another log reveals this phase in process:

> On my second reading, I tried to focus on the content of "Thanatopsis." Unable to define the title, I went to the footnote.

Classmates hearing this would be reminded that effective readers attend to titles and the meanings of unknown words. Although teacherly reminders of such strategies are frequent, they often fall on deaf ears, which receive messages much more readily from peer voices.

Definition is typically coupled with an exploration during which a reader supplements and reinforces the quest for evidence on which to ground the hypothesis. Questions continue to surface as the reader seeks to collect and present the evidence relating to the hypothesis:

> The first line tells who this poem is for. It says "To him who in the love of Nature holds. . . . " I understood that lover of Nature, however simple he was described, would be buried with patriarchs, kings and so on. I did not understand lines 60–64 for it talks about other people. Who are they? What do they symbolize?

Generating questions, a reader can return to the text for evidence that might suggest some answers.

Eventually, the reader, satisfied with the results of his or her exploration, accepts the hypothesis as a demonstrated conclusion and moves to the last phase of critical inquiry: generalization.

The following process log, presented in its entirety, demonstrates the progression from phase to phase that this student experienced reading the poem:

> When I first read through the poem, my reaction was "Whaaat!?" I understood from about the second stanza on that he was talking generally about death, but I couldn't understand the details. I slowed down a bit and it helped [*orientation*]. The free verse kind of threw me because there was no rhyme so I started pausing at each punctuation mark [*hypothesis*]. That was a definite helper. I got to the end with relief but also with a feeling like a bucket of water had been thrown on my head. With highlighter in hand I sat down to read it again and conquer the poem.
>
> As I went line by line I guess I caught this guy's style because something clicked and I was off and running. I underlined all the important words and wrote what I thought he was saying in the margins [*hypothesis and exploration*]. When I finished the poem looked like an ink bomb had gone off but I also felt comfortable with the poem and its meanings [*generalization*].
>
> The third time around I read for symbolism and feelings and was blown away. I loved the way he put some things—like "to be a brother to the insensible rock" and "all in one mighty sepulchre" [*evidence*]. He made death sound exciting and something to look forward to. It wasn't that you were leaving earth but that you were going to somewhere new to join thousands of ancient famous people [*generalization*]. I felt happy for all those who had died and looked forward to meeting them. The idea of no God there didn't seem to bother me. I would send this kind of hopeful poem to my dying relatives if I didn't think it would offend them, because dying is scary and this poem takes a little of the fear away.

As might be expected, the phases of such inquiry are recursive. Beginning with one very personal (but intellectual) orientation ("Whaaat?"—i.e., what does this mean?), the student ended with another, quite different, orientation, grounded in both understanding and feeling.

The writer's language reveals the sense of adventure that this process of engagement generates ("I sat down to read it again and conquer the poem"). Envisioning the reader as conquering hero, the student donned a cloak of swashbuckling confidence and was "off and running." Fighting the initial violence that the poem inflicted on him (his "feeling like a bucket of water had been thrown on [his] head"), this reader assumed an offensive stance and exploded personalized "ink bombs" to subdue the text.

Confident and self-assured ("I felt comfortable with the poem and its meanings"), the student then entered the poem a third time and was willingly "blown away" as the poem continued to unfold its language and its vision. Composing meanings from literature can be a struggle for domination between self and text. The volley between this writer and the poem suggests a proper balance of power developing.

Process logs not only disclose students' movement through the phases of analytical inquiry, they serve to give students confidence. Students learn they cannot expect full comprehension on their first readings. They learn that, as they continue to work with a piece, they will understand more and more. Their personal experiences with a text are validated and extended by sharing logs with fellow classmates. Literary encounters become adventurous challenges potent for success, not disastrous invasions predestined to fail.

The value of developing student confidence must not be underestimated. Good readers are confident. Poor ones are not. Where are we to draw the line between cause and effect? The process log, like the dialogue journal, explicitly allows students to be tentative and uncertain. Free to fail, they are likely to succeed instead.

Reading competence, structuralist critics would suggest, is dependent upon a system of conventions that readers bring to texts (Culler 1980, 102). Process logs help students examine their conventions and revise them as needed. The conventions of postmodern narrative (the fragmentation of time and space, the layering of meanings, and the consciousness of self as verbal text, for example) are not the conventions of earlier narrative. Readers coming to texts with inappropriate conventions are doomed to the frustration of inadequate readings unless they can revise their reading strategies.

Similarly, students who encounter "Thanatopsis" with the expectation that the end of a line will signal the end of a meaning unit find themselves perplexed. Revising strategies, they apply a reading convention appropriate for blank verse (that is, they use regular sentence capitalization and punctuation instead of line endings to signal meaning units). Only then are they able to make sense of their reading. By making the revision of strategy explicit, a process log makes it accessible to other students in the class who encounter similar difficulties but are less successful in their responses.

The Structuralist understanding of the importance of genre conventions suggests that, with process logs, we are not simply teaching reading skills. Understanding that literary texts insist on a variety of interpretive operations makes students more open to texts that are difficult to process with familiar strategies. This readerly openness becomes a first step to growth, knowledge, and literary competence—the fluent use of reading conventions. Helping students recognize the demands of different literary structures helps them see relationships between and among texts. We are not just teaching facts or techniques but patterns of response that students can transfer to a wide range of texts.

In addition to teaching literary structure and the reading conventions that each demands, process logs teach students patterns of perception. Perception is clearly at the heart of composing meaning. As our perceptions are limited, so are our explanations. For Jerome Bruner, perceptual unreadiness results either from inappropriate categories or from an inadequate range of categories available for coding and processing data (1957, 128–29).

Experience with the writing and sharing of process logs enables students to broaden their range of available classification categories. In their logs, they practice category application, and the rapid feedback provided by class discussion allows them to evaluate equally rapidly the efficacy of their category choices.[1] Thus, much of the power of the process log lies in its conscious revelation and extension of both perception and the meanings composed thereby.

By asking students to write about their processes of composing meaning, we are disturbing an automatic activity. Vygotsky asserts that such "disturbance in an automatic activity makes the [composer] aware of this activity" (1986, 30). He elaborates on the value of such awareness:

> In perceiving some of our acts in a generalized fashion, we isolate them from our total mental activity and are thus enabled to focus on this process as such and to enter into a new relation to it. In this way, becoming conscious of our operations and viewing each as a process of a certain *kind*... leads to their mastery. (170–71)

Again, we are not teaching skills but self-awareness of thinking processes. Once students are aware of what they do when faced with literary problems (such as the fragmented prose of *The Sound and the Fury,* the complex allusions of *The Waste Land,* or the multiple narrative voices of *Ulysses*), they begin to see what they might do. The process log offers not only a record of a past encounter with a text but potential direction for reencounter. In addition, it provides a tool for teacher analysis of student process. As students reveal their methods of reading, we can suggest alternate modes of productive response.

Confidence, recognition of structure and convention, enhanced perception, and self-awareness are all important to developing readers. Both the dialogue journal and the process log show us how we can teach students to use language to distance themselves from their perceptions, feelings, and thoughts about a text. Both serve to remind us of the closely knit relationship between thinking and using language.

5 Writing About Texts: Reading Responses

The reading response is a form that is flexible and easy enough to be used by any student capable of forming sentences with moderate fluency. Usually, it involves asking students to freewrite for ten to twenty minutes in response to whatever reading they have just completed. While teachers need to set a time limit appropriate to student abilities (experience suggests anything less than ten minutes is not productive), the task requires no particular level of literary sophistication. Typically, the only training students need involves learning to freewrite.

I use *freewriting* quite specifically here (and throughout this book) to mean beginning to write and continuing to write steadily for a predetermined period of time without stopping for correction or reflection. The writer cannot finish before the time is up but must continue to put words on the page. The writing is intended to generate meanings rather than to express preshaped thoughts. The idea is to connect the flow of thinking and writing so directly that the latter enables the former.

The words "in response" explicitly position the reader as a receiver of the text while calling for an expression of his or her response to it. "Response" is open enough to include many appropriate possibilities that might be subjective, objective, emotional, intellectual, or combinations thereof, including reaction, description, summary, comment, analysis, and synthesis. Asking students to respond to the reading they "have just completed," suggests the existence of past and potential readings—readings done either at different times or by other people. The invitation to write is located both temporally and subjectively and is therefore receptive to potential expansion and revision.

The reading response is freer in both form and focus than either the dialogue journal or the process log (although the assignment can be focused productively to suit specific pedagogical or critical purposes, as I will discuss later in this chapter). In some ways, the reading response synthesizes the other two modes. The focus is not simply on what a reader noticed in the text (as in the dialogue journal, chapter 3) or on how a reader noticed (as in the process log, chapter 4). Instead, attention shifts to the meanings generated by both of these. In a reading response, the emphasis is on an interpretation and evaluation—the results of the generative tensions between text and reader.

Students often begin reading responses with highly valuative reactions and then move to explore those reactions. The opening lines of the two reading responses that follow are typical of those written by high-school juniors and seniors. The first is part of a response to two poems by Anne Bradstreet, "The Prologue" and "The Author to Her Book."

> Among the colonial authors I've read so far (not too many), Bradstreet is the wittiest, best of them yet. Her pieces are easy to relate to, as compared to Bradford's "Plantation."

This writer (a young woman) identified two qualities of Bradstreet's work—wit and ease of connection—that helped her rank Bradstreet's work above others. By articulating matters of personal taste of which she may not have been aware, her response to other colonial writers (ranked lower) became transparent and available for evaluation. She (or a peer, or a teacher) could then question her initial responses, allowing her to consider revising them according to other criteria.

Another student (a young man) had a more emotional reaction in his response to Katherine Anne Porter's "Flowering Judas."

> The main thing that pops into my head about this story is that I hate it. I found it very confusing and so I couldn't get into it. Therefore, to me it was extremely boring.

This student articulated both an emotional and an intellectual response ("I hate it" and "it was extremely boring"), and his use of "therefore" suggests his recognition that confusion was central to his strong dislike of this story. Unable to find coherent meaning, he aimed the anger and annoyance caused by his failure at the text.

The remainder of his reading response pushes to identify anything that makes sense. "I suppose that this story is supposed to parallel the story of Judas," he notes grudgingly. He then observes that the theme of forgiveness connects both Judas and Braggioni's wife. Having started in this direction, the writer eventually identifies Laura (as the betrayer of Eugenio) with Judas.

Putting his anger behind, this student grew willing (and able) to return to the text several times to find what he could productively say about it in spite of his initial confusion. He didn't just reject the text because of a hostility generated by confusion. Had he done so, the text would have remained opaque. Because the reading response accepts hostility, boredom, and confusion as legitimate reactions to texts, it diffuses the power of such negative emotions. Students are free to operate more analytically once their emotions have been released.

While there is much more to be addressed in the text than this student managed in a fifteen-minute reading response, his emotional response propelled him toward some useful first statements. His reading response reveals energy and the creative thinking that is central to critical inquiry (I am using "creative thinking" here to describe the production of an idea new to its creator). He accomplished a great deal in only fifteen minutes of writing.

The activity of making meaning from texts is both emotionally and intellectually grounded. New perceptual experience generates an instantaneous (although often unnoticed) emotional response. Readings that ignore emotional responses are inadequate, because they acknowledge only half the literary transaction. Such readings look only at how a reader touches a text and are insensitive to how a text touches its readers. Such insensitivity, logically enough, constrains the capacity for full exploration; our reading and our teaching become clumsy if we plunge into literary analysis before first allowing students (or ourselves) full opportunity to recognize highly personal, often emotional, experiences with texts. We can use these emotional responses not only as a starting point from which to begin discussion but also to help students create knowledge about themselves as readers; such responses reveal the ways in which texts act upon readers and readers act upon texts as readers work toward composing coherent and satisfactory meanings.

The reading response also gives students an opportunity to connect reading with personal experience. Here is the opening paragraph of a student's reading response to E. M. Forster's "The Road from Colonus":

> This was a pretty sad story. I have compassion for Mr. Lucas because he doesn't want to be old but he can't help it. It makes me think of how my grandparents must feel and how I may feel at that time.

Emotional connections should not be undervalued or labeled frivolous. A work that fails to move us also fails to compel our attention and will quickly fade from view.

Sometimes, a personal connection to a text is couched in intellectual rather than emotional terms, as seen in this response to Poe's "Fall of the House of Usher":

> Gothic. Definitely complex sentence structure. The only reason that I can read it at all is that I had four years of Caesar and Cicero (who by the way is worse). A lot of mixed word order according to the effect needed. Impact and suspense require different formats, and Poe uses placement of verbs and phrases to speed up or slow down time's passage as he wishes.

Not only is this student able to connect Poe's complexity of style to similar complexity in Latin texts, but his tone suggests the pleasure he finds in dealing with a style that is difficult but manageable for him because of his prior experience. To prove his mastery over the text, he makes some rather sophisticated observations about the relationships between the form and function of language and particularly about Poe's mimetic use of language to reflect the passage of time.

The reading response provides a regular means by which students are enabled to make both connections and discoveries about their reading because it shapes and focuses the chaos of random thought, both spatially and temporally. The writing flow helps students generate connections. Once the connections are objectified on the page, they become available to the writer for analysis. Students can distance themselves from responses enough to recognize (and understand) their implications. Regular writing about reading thus engages students in acts of active perception and reflection, helping them discover patterns, connections, and meanings in texts and pushing them from the emotional and experiential to the analytical and conceptual.

The following reading response was written by a high-school senior after reading Erskine Caldwell's "The Warm River." It is typical of what many students write after a few weeks of practice with this form. The writer (a young woman) began with summary.

> The story line is basic, a man [Richard] who goes to visit his sweetheart, yet intends to leave her and not marry her as she hopes he will. But something happens to make him change his mind; when he sees her sobbing, he realizes he "loves" her, loves her in the way her father loved her mother, and decides to stay.

Plot summation is a common beginning move in reading responses. It provides writers with a way to get the business of proving they understood what happened out of the way quickly and efficiently and then to move on to response and analysis.

Having summarized, this writer was ready for a more personal response. Recognizing her dissatisfaction with elements of the story, she struggled to understand her reasons for displeasure.

> Okay. That's sweet. But I do not feel happy at the end of the story. I guess it's because I'm not convinced his love *is* real love. Why? I'm not sure. Maybe because he was so callously going to leave her, and had just come to hold her for an hour. Perhaps I felt that this was using her, showing her emotions no respect.

The outcome of the story disturbed this writer on a personal level. For her, the young man's change of heart was not presented convincingly. The phrase "showing her emotions no respect" suggests an area in which the writer felt potentially threatened herself.

In her next paragraph, the writer attempted to reconcile her feelings:

> But at the same time, these gut feelings could be wrong. Perhaps he really loves her, and his journey was one of discovery, realization, or awakening of feeling. Perhaps he was coming to terms with some fear, some hang-up he had that was restricting his giving of love.

The reading response allowed this student to become a reader of her own text. Having engaged in what I. A. Richards calls an "audit of meaning" (1958, 240), she was able to achieve critical distance and discover an alternative interpretation.

Writing in this way forces students to recognize that texts have many potential meanings; as they see the development of their ideas, they see possibilities for revision. After careful perception, a reader moves beyond the limits of the individual landscape. This movement—from personal textual experience to less personal analytical distance—is central to critical inquiry. It enables a panoptic vision that reaches toward universal horizons.

In this particular reading response, the student's horizons continued to expand. Having exhausted discussion of her dissatisfaction with Richard's behavior, she assumed a more traditionally critical approach and sought to explore the symbolic values of the story, working to find a coherent and personally satisfying reading:

> In this way the river could be considered symbolic. When he first arrives, crossing the bridge is terrifying, harrowing; he has a great fear of "falling" off the rickety bridge, which he is not used to. So he tries

> to outrun it, run away. This could be a parallel to his fear of love (the girl, the river) and how he is trying to run away. As they tell him later in the story, "It is something you must learn to accept, get used to, and it will not be as frightening." The warmth of the river, then, would be the warmth of love that the girl can give him and the warmth of his own love he is afraid to give. When he begins to accept his love for the girl is when he begins to see the river in a new light, not as something to fear, but as something good. When he asks her to take him down to the river after he tells her he is staying, is when he has come to terms with his feelings, and is ready to accept them with open arms, and even go so far as exploring them.

The writer's willingness to speculate, to explore the possibility that her initial response might have been unfair or limiting, generated her hypothesis that the young man could be understood differently if viewed as being on a journey of discovery. This hypothesis, and her testing of it, enable her to come to terms with symbolic levels of the text in satisfying ways.

In addition to providing a way for students to examine and revise initial reactions, reading responses invite explicit questioning of texts. In a reading response to "Flowering Judas," one student listed the following questions:

> What significance does the singing of Braggioni have to the story?
> What is going on with Laura in the beginning portion of the story?
> What significance is there in the dream at the end of the story?

Another student, responding to "The Cask of Amontillado," wondered why Poe set his story in Europe (especially since the event that inspired the tale took place in New Jersey) and remarked that it "seems odd for an American writer" to do so. A third student wondered about Hemingway's use of drinks in "Hills Like White Elephants," commenting that they "must have had something to do with the story, but I'm not sure exactly what."

These gaps in understanding—what Tom Newkirk calls the "incoherencies in a reading" (1990, 210)—are central to the process of critical inquiry, but too often students (and teachers?) see them as failures rather than as opportunities. Without incoherencies, the generation of critical questions is unlikely. One could, in fact, suggest that a totally coherent reading—that is, one that claims to close all gaps and admits no questions—is inadequate in a most fundamental way.

A value of such gaps, both for readers and for teachers of literature, rests in their indeterminacy. Gaps will be different for different readers; they will be filled in various ways. Inherent in their indeterminacy is the potential for each reading to generate new lines of critical inquiry that can contribute productively to textual discussion. What we and our students know about a text is often not as useful as what makes us uncertain.

Each incoherence provides a potential signpost, pointing toward a coherent reading of a text. This directional value of incoherence is observable in the following excerpt from another student's reading response to "Warm River":

> That's when I'm confused. It seemed that in the beginning he [Richard] had come because he was physically attracted to Gretchen. Realizing this he cannot tell her he loves her "just a little" or explain his feelings.
>
> The river seems to separate Gretchen and her family from the outside world. It seems to protect them too because its warm mists come to the house. Even in winter the river doesn't freeze over but remains warm. I really don't know what the river symbolizes. Love? Love for their mother? Since it always flows. But how does the river tell Richard that he really does love Gretchen?

Statement of one question ("Love?") led to the generation of evidence and a second question ("But how does the river tell Richard . . . ?"). Unhappily, rather than having followed the potential line of inquiry further, the student collapsed into a sense of inadequacy, which she transferred to the text ("Gee, the stories are getting harder"), and stopped writing.

One hopes that, with coaching and increased confidence, such a student might come to understand with Francis Christiansen that "the mere form of the sentence generates ideas" (1983, 177). Trusting in the powerful ability of language to generate and develop thought (rather than merely to express it), a reader is no longer overwhelmed by the many questions that any careful reading arouses but willing instead to use written language to push toward the satisfaction of making meaning.

In addition to helping students generate meaning, writing reading responses may enable them to gain access to what Kenneth Burke calls "the recallable but not explicitly recalled," by which he means "knowledge which one has, but which does not happen to be associated with the given topic under discussion" (1966, 72). Most often, such access is signaled by a student making connections between the current text and another, or between text and context, as in the following reading response to Benjamin Franklin's *Autobiography*:

> When I first started to read . . . the first thing that came to my mind was the similarity of his writing to that of Addison and Steele. I hadn't realized that, while England had that period of Enlightenment . . . America was greatly influenced by that era's beliefs as well. Having taken British literature, I know that they believed greatly in knowledge and manners. Franklin sounded incredibly English to me in that sense.

Such connections are, of course, enormously valuable, both to student and teacher, and again illustrate what I mean by creative thinking: thoughts new to the thinker. To a teacher, the connection between England and America (and even that between Franklin and Addison and Steele) seems obvious, but it is not as obvious as we may think and, once articulated, provided this student with an important and useful frame for further literary studies.

The reading response provides one final value in a literature class. During the act of reading, the thoughts, feelings, language of another being enter our minds, and we willingly submit to their influence, often adapting and adopting them for our own uses. Occasionally, a reading response makes such importation visible and accessible to analysis.

In the following reading response to several essays by Emerson, the writer imported Emerson's words into her text and then juxtaposed her language to his:

> This selection showed me how true it is that we think of Fate as a limitation. Anything "wrong" which comes from Nature, we call Fate.

> "A part of Fate is the freedom of man." We can choose what we do with what is presented to us.
>
> "So far as man thinks, he is free." Again, I find this very similar to Socrates. I also noticed Emerson's use of the "link in a chain" when he says man is not free. Is this a reference to Pope's *Essay on Man?*

Putting Emerson's language into her own text enabled this writer to paraphrase and evaluate comfortably, as well as to extend a series of philosophical connections that link Pope and Socrates with Emerson and, eventually, her own beliefs.

For another student, importation caused him to raise a question about the attitude toward women that Anne Bradstreet expresses:

> In "The Prologue," Bradstreet helps us understand the society in which women were simply thought of as wives or mothers. She was very conspicuous as a woman poet in those days, and she knows that men might look down on her poetry because it was written by a woman. She humbles herself, and women in general in this poem. ("Men can do best; women know it well.") The part that got me the most though, was in the last stanza. "This mean and unrefined ore of mine/will make your glistening gold but more to shine." Perhaps she meant it, but perhaps it also struck out at men in the colonial times, putting them on a guilt trip about the role given to women.

Once this student had imported parts of Bradstreet's text into his own, he examined them for undercurrents. Does Bradstreet believe her words or is something else at work here, he wondered? Having submitted to Bradstreet's text as a reader, he then acted on it as a writer. The reading response made his action available both to himself and to any others with whom he shared it. Temporarily frozen by the act of writing, the literary experience becomes an available subject for discussion.

Up to now, I have been describing free reading responses, where the directions ask students to focus on a text in a general way. However, it is perfectly appropriate, and often quite useful, for a teacher to alter these directions somewhat to direct students' attention to a particular aspect of a text. For example:

- In your reading response to "Bartleby the Scrivener" include consideration of why Bartleby always says, "I would prefer not to."

These directions prepare students for a discussion that will examine the implications of the word "prefer" and, by extension, the nature of free choice in Melville's story. Other directions provide starting points for different kinds of discussion. For example:

- In your reading response to "The Fall of the House of Usher," think about the different settings in this story, the effects of each, and any symbolic functions of setting that you can identify.

The reading response students write when guided by these directions focuses discussion on fictional strategies rather than on thematic issues; background elements of the tale (setting rather than plot or characters) are brought to the foreground of student attention.

The next set of directions serves a different function:

- Do one reading response for all the Sandburg poems. Think about what Sandburg owes to Whitman in terms of content and style. Try to make as many specific comments and references to the poems as you can.

Often, students see works or writers in isolation and need guidance to make necessary connections. The agenda underpinning these instructions is to have students trace a line of influence from one poet to another.

When using focused reading responses, teachers need to make it clear that students should not feel limited by the particular direction suggested. As in any response, they are still free to comment on whatever interests them; they are simply asked to include consideration of a particular issue in their overall remarks.

Whether we use free or focused reading responses, we must remember that response statements are a means to an end, not the end itself. The students' writing is only a first step. The teacher and the class must receive and use that writing in some real and productive way. Each reading response needs to become part of the intertextuality of class discussion encompassing both literary and student texts, one more aspect of the ongoing classroom discourse about texts. Here are some ways in which reading responses can be integrated with discussion.

At the beginning of discussion, a student reads a reading response aloud. The class listens and jots down comments or questions that the reading response raises. At the end of the oral reading, the teacher or a student summarizes and focuses the initial discussion. For example:

> I heard Greg wondering about the lines, "Men can do best; women know it well" and "This mean and unrefined ore of mine/will make your glistening gold but more to shine." What useful comments or observations can we make about those lines?

or

> Chris was wondering about the relationships between the river and love. Let's start our discussion by exploring that issue.

The conversation begins with a student's text and with a student's concerns.

What are the values of having students share their reading responses with one another? Foremost, students validate their feelings and ideas by hearing them from others. This validation is especially important to those who are uncertain of their abilities and who view themselves as apprentices. Repeated experiences with shared responses build a foundation of trust in their readings that enables students to attempt more daring critical structures.

By making student writing part of the critical conversation, we force students to expand the range of their thinking by engaging with a wider public. Group conversation teaches them to evaluate, assimilate, and respond to the ideas expressed by others and protects them from simply echoing the voices of established critical authority. Not only do we expand students' frames of reference by group sharing, we also expand the group's reading of a specific text.

The experience is essentially dialectic. Each reader shares an individual response that is different from all the others. Each response presents the group with a new view of the text that they have all been sharing. This dialectical sharing is what leads the community as a group toward what David Bleich calls "interpretive validity."

These dialectical experiences are within a teacher's direction. Teachers have agendas, no matter how collaborative the classroom. With any literary text in the context of any literature course, there are issues that we wish the class to address. My experience suggests, however, that, when given the opportunity, students typically raise most of the issues on such an agenda without any prompting from the teacher. As discussion of the first reading response is exhausted, the class moves on to another and then another. If a particular issue has not surfaced by the end of the allotted time, I simply summarize the discussion thus far and raise the issue myself; for example:

> So far in our discussion of some of the parallel or recurring events in *Huckleberry Finn* we have talked about Tom's behavior at the beginning and the end of the book, we have talked about the ways Huck gets information when he arrives in a new community and how he uses it to his advantage, and we've discussed occurrences of disguise, costumes, and play acting. Perhaps this is a good time for us to explore the different scams that occur throughout the novel and to take a look at what Twain seems to be doing with them. Did anyone consider scams in his or her reading response?

Another way to achieve this same end is to cross-fertilize with comments from other classes:

> Last period's class mentioned the issues you have; they also talked about the scams in the novel. Did anyone in this class get around to mentioning that?

While the discussion is student centered, it is (as it should be) teacher directed.

Reading responses can also work within small groups. Four or five students share their reading responses, discuss them, and then report to the entire class on key points or central questions that need to be addressed. Or each student shares his or her reading response with a partner, working together to produce a collective list of questions raised by the text for the class to consider. This is often a useful way to begin the discussion of a novel, for example.

A group lists questions on an overhead transparency or on a large sheet of newsprint, which is then posted in the room; the class agenda becomes visible and remains accessible. If more than one class is studying the same work, so much the better: the various lists work to inform one another and to enlarge the critical community beyond a particular course section.

When a teacher begins a class with a list of prepared questions, the pattern of the ensuing discussion is linear and relatively predictable. Using student reading responses as the basis for textual exploration is messier. A teacher cannot foretell the starting point (although a quick preview of reading responses before discussion begins could allow one to stack the deck) or the ways in which the group will move from one issue to the next. Two classes will shape their discussions of the same issues in radically different ways. Teachers need new management strategies in order to keep track of what has and has not been said. This is easier than it may at first appear.

Freed from the responsibility of generating extensive lists of discussion questions, the teacher can focus more directly on the text and ask what central issues a particular text potentially raises for a class at a given point in their development. In fact, a teacher might well write a reading response as a means of exploring the text personally for answers to this question. Answers will be shaped by student abilities and interests, course focus and goals, and, quite possibly, by teacherly predilections. Whatever the response, the teacher can use it to select issues and passages to center class focus. Here is a list of central issues and passages from Bret Harte's story "The Outcasts of Poker Flat" that might be used for an average high-school class:

- Piney and Tom's effect on the behavior of the other characters.
- Mother Shipman's decision to starve herself for Piney.
- Mr. Oakhurst's feelings for the Duchess.
- Oakhurst "who was at once the strongest and the weakest of the outcasts of Poker Flat."

Were the story taught for a different purpose, different issues might be appropriate.

- The conventions of local-color writing.
- Bret Harte's development of the humorous aspects of this story.
- The combination of humor and death and how it works.
- Sentimentality.

None of these issues allows single statement; each serves as the nucleus for a cluster of possible commentary. Furthermore, each list reveals a different pedagogical agenda.

For the teacher, the list becomes a checklist to use during discussion. As members of the class raise an issue or refer to a passage, the teacher notes this on the list. In addition, the teacher adds to the list issues of importance that the class raises but the teacher hasn't previously noted. As a class session nears its end, a quick review of the list enables the teacher to bring up for discussion any issue that the class has not generated itself.

This sort of textual exploration is not freewheeling, although it is free-form. Students do not say just anything in any order. The class goal is collaborative discussion of those issues that the group feels are important, with an eye toward developing a reading of the text at hand that is satisfying to all. The teacher, as a member of the community, has not only the right but the responsibility to help define the list of issues and to contribute to the shaping of the community reading.

Important from an educational point of view, using the reading response to start discussion properly puts responsibility on students. They generate questions. They raise and discuss issues, testing readings among themselves. They determine the order of discussion. As a result, they become responsible for owning their texts as well as their readings. Ultimately, the real value lies in that ownership, for without the confidence of ownership, students are unable to clear the imaginative space demanded by critical composition.

CONCLUSION

Dialogue journals, process logs, and reading responses provide ways for students to connect with texts and to increase their powers of perception. These connections and perceptions are both personal and communal, made individually and shared collaboratively with classmates.

These three modes of response assume that reading, responding, and composing are all aspects of understanding, each of which can only be understood in relation to the others. With each mode, texts are understood to generate interactions as their readers compose meanings. Meanings are understood to gain validity through the collaborative interchanges of the critical community formed by the literature class.

Literature is more than a body of knowledge. It creates the potential for both aesthetic and critical experience. In our teaching, we seek to give students rich literary experience and engaged critical discussion. To that end, we use dialogue journals, process logs, and reading responses to integrate reading, writing, and classroom discussion in a process of critical inquiry.

These response modes have practical value as well as theoretical validity for both teacher and student. For the teacher, they are flexible; they can be adapted to suit specific course objectives and specific student groups. They can be used singly or in sequence. Once students learn the forms, they can use them repeatedly throughout a course. Requiring little teacher direction after a period of initial training, they demand a high level of student involvement.

These modes enable us to free ourselves from our once-primary roles as either police or evaluators. Students cannot write a dialogue journal or a process log or a reading response without doing the reading. Thus, we no longer have to give reading quizzes, which often inadequately check on whether or not a student has read an assignment. (We all know of students who pass our quizzes after discussing the reading with a classmate or those who are diligent readers but whose patterns of textual observation make it impossible for them to respond appropriately to the quiz questions we choose.) These response forms cannot be copied because the individual voice that each student quickly develops makes them highly idiosyncratic. Because these modes are teaching/learning tools, we need not grade them; we simply give them credit/no credit points. Evaluation of these modes is properly restricted to analysis of our students' display of their composing processes as readers and writers.

Since these modes are personal, we should ignore spelling and other mechanical errors. In fact, when we ask students to freewrite, we are *insisting* that they not stop to edit; having so insisted, we would be unfair to penalize them for following our directions. These modes focus on the exploration of texts and the composition of meanings; our responses should have a similar focus. Our feedback should be designed to help students evaluate their performances accurately. Figures 1 and 2 reproduce sample reading responses with my feedback. As you can see, while the feedback is brief, it is chatty, personal, and designed to be helpful.

Teacher commentary should be a learning prompt, offered for its value to the student and designed to help the student see strengths and false steps in a textual response. By refusing to perform as evaluators, we have full capacity to act as mentors, instead.

Readers may begin to wonder about the logistics of dealing with increased amounts of student writing. The key is to give feedback rather than grades. Feedback can come from teachers or peers; it can come as a group response to writing shared aloud or simply by having one's thoughts validated and expanded in the course of class discussion. If a teacher wishes, students can assemble all the dialogue logs, process journals, and reading responses written during a unit or grading period into a reader's notebook, numbering pages, writing titles for each entry, providing a table of contents, and writing a valuative summary or conclusion to the work as a whole.

Another approach would have students choose several pieces and find a way to combine them into a single, unified essay (clearly, this is easiest for students when the various pieces are all based on the same work or the same author). When extensive student writing becomes burdensome to a teacher, a revision of management techniques generally provides relief.

Dialogue journals, process logs, and reading responses provide teachers with invaluable access to the ways in which students compose. We can see *how* they read and *how* they write. When students mine texts richly, we can reveal to them the critical conventions that they apply and their usefulness. When they stray far from the text, we can help them see how their thinking lost its center.

We might show students how they move from literal levels of comprehension—such as finding basic stated information, identifying key details, and noting stated relationships—to inferential levels of comprehension—such as recognizing simple and complex implied relationships, stating author's generalizations, and identifying structural generalizations. As we make student strategies transparent, our identifications and labelings help students gain control over their own processes. Process and product naturally combine as topics of classroom discussion, and students see how each determines and shapes the other.

As we see what students *are* doing with their texts, we can lead (or push) them toward what they *can* do. As they share processes with one another, students are introduced to new strategies to use with texts, new questions to pose while reading. Often, all a teacher needs to do is identify what one member of the group has done and offer it to the class as a possible mode of action. Real changes in the reading/composing powers of the

Reading Response pp. 60--86

I'm having some difficulty responding to this section because I didn't read the entire section in one sitting. I know—bad move.

Sometimes it's hard to avoid — ☺!

The first section of this section (pp. 60-65) introduced a more mature Stephen. He is more aware of his surroundings like his detection of the changes in his house, but he is as deeply involved in his thoughts as ever. Stephen not only reads books, but he becomes the character in the book—The Count of Monte Cristo. ✓

I had difficulty interpretting the following section (pp. 65-72) Stephen's family (is forced?) to move—financial difficulties? yes He then spends time visiting his mother's relatives, but is disturbed by "his mood of embittered silence" (67). I understand (or rather, have ideas) why he is melancholy. But why are these visitation scenes significant? Who's Ellen, the elderly lady? Yes, I realize Eileen is the one whom Stephen (loves? —too strong an emotion?) is infatuated with — Also, what effect does Mr. Dedalus's

Figure 1 Reading Response to *A Portrait of the Artist as a Young Man*, pp. 60–86

group grow collaboratively from the strengths of individual members.

Using dialogue journals, process logs, and reading responses as starting points for class discussion expands the audience for student writing. Students no longer write for a teacher but for a

S—

Hmm - good point -

treatment of the Stephen / Fr Dolan incident have on Stephen?

In the following section (pp. 73–86) I was surprised at Stephen's maturity. Did we jump ahead a few years? yes He is one of the oldest boys and a leader at his school. When I compared Stephen to his rival Heron, he was much more sensitive. Stephen is now aware of each situation — at least more than in the first school scenes. He stands his ground in his own way — either doesn't "admit" or avoids confrontation. He also takes literature seriously, but rebels (cautiously) against religion. I saw this in his favoring Byron over Tennyson. On pp. 83–84, Stephen is described as hearing "hollowsounding voices" which he wishes to avoid. The final scene describes a dissappointed Stephen who is upset over not seeing Eileen(?). He is developing into the sensitive, disturbed young artist (I like the last paragraph on pg. 78 — from "this sensitive nature" until "into his crude writings.")

Good

community. As a result, their interest in their writing grows beyond the limits of details of presentation (such as handwriting, spelling, and punctuation) and the teacher's grade on the piece. Writing becomes a way of making and conveying meanings in a real, social context. School writing grows more nearly to approximate

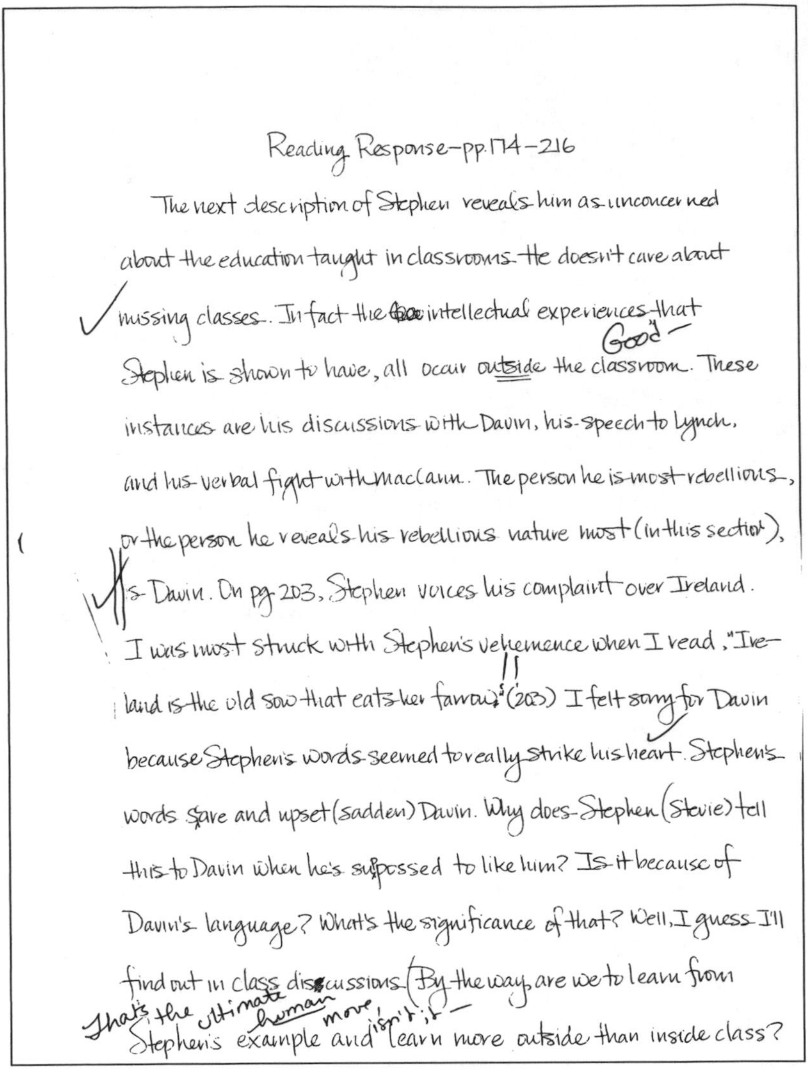

Reading Response—pp.174–216

The next description of Stephen reveals him as unconcerned about the education taught in classrooms. He doesn't care about missing classes. In fact the intellectual experiences that Stephen is shown to have, all occur outside the classroom. Good— These instances are his discussions with Davin, his speech to Lynch, and his verbal fight with MacCann. The person he is most rebellious, or the person he reveals his rebellious nature most (in this section), is Davin. On pg 203, Stephen voices his complaint over Ireland. I was most struck with Stephen's vehemence when I read, "Ireland is the old sow that eats her farrow" (203) I felt sorry for Davin because Stephen's words seemed to really strike his heart. Stephen's words scare and upset (sadden) Davin. Why does Stephen (Stevie) tell this to Davin when he's supossed to like him? Is it because of Davin's language? What's the significance of that? Well, I guess I'll find out in class discussions. (By the way, are we to learn from Stephen's example and learn more outside than inside class?

That's the ultimate human move, isn't it—

Figure 2 Reading Response to *A Portrait of the Artist as a Young Man,* pp. 174–216

the demands of real-world writing because students must consider a real audience. They learn to write for an audience of variously skeptical readers rather than for one well-known individual (the teacher). Writing successfully for a real audience of informed, judgmental peers demands thoughtful explorations of meaning. Using

S——

Only kidding?) It is Davin's story of the seducing peasant woman that also sticks in Stephen's mind. His Stephen's attitude towards women is definitely interesting. At the very ending of this section, we see Stephen's "beloved." He shuns even her because he mistrusts her friendliness to a priest. Does Stephen see women as cheap? But then what about the beautiful girl on the beach? Is she "human" or a romantic image? — Stephen's discussion about beauty and art was a little contrived in my opinion. Like we mentioned in class, too rhetorical. As a young artist, I suppose Stephen is trying to be constantly eloquent. His battle with MacCann was also interesting. Everyone crowds round to hear the intellectual fight between conformists and non-conformist. I'm quite sure there's a lot in this section that I missed.

Another question: Why does Cranly always speak Latin? Or is it Latin? And what's he saying? yes – They are both showing off – I can figure out the short responses, but the long ones mean nothing to me? Is he trying to be an ultra-intellectual also? ✓

the three response modes presented in this section enables some important first steps in such exploration.

Dialogue journals, process logs, and reading responses are composing modes that have enormous value to the student as well. They are useful instruments with which to see and express knowledge on a habitual basis. Once the forms are learned and practiced, they can be used independently of a teacher or a class. Personally useful to a reader engaging with a text, they have potential value as composing strategies for individual use outside an academic setting.

These exploratory discourse modes help students learn about the power of language itself. They learn what Ann Berthoff calls "the uses of chaos" (1981, 38). As they struggle to resolve the incoherences of their readings, they use language to shape their reading experiences. They find that writing helps them locate and retrieve information from long-term memory that might otherwise have been inaccessible to their reading of a particular text. They learn to use the generative powers of language.

A student's private withdrawal to write eventually enables his or her participation in a collaborative, critical conversation. Students are freed from the limiting tyranny of single textual meaning and their accompanying need to be right about a text. Recognizing that any text provides legitimate opportunities for numerous useful comments and gaining confidence in their own abilities as readers, students learn to use writing to clear the space they need for their own creative, critical acts. Having reconstructed textual meanings and developed their own ideas about their readings, students are ready to refocus those ideas for other readers.

TEACHING CRITICAL DISTANCE

INTRODUCTION

Although the writing activities of the first section help students gain confidence in their abilities to speak in a collective voice, teaching students to become good literary critics is still difficult because of the academic conventions that narrowly define the range of forms available for critical use. Interestingly, this narrow focus holds strong at the very time when possible imaginative forms are expanding. Our poets, dramatists, and novelists are working with self-conscious, formal experimentation, while in many classrooms, even at the university level, we continue to insist that public response to literature can be shaped properly only in the thesis-driven argument essay. Unhappily, the formal limitations we have imposed upon ourselves severely restrict our abilities as teachers and equally inhibit the critical discourse of our students.

In literary criticism, argument, as a form, is in direct conflict with the nature of the aesthetic experience to which it attempts to respond. Argument posits singularity and certainty; literary experience is multifarious and contingent. Argument and the insistence on logical proof that it implies suggest a correspondingly intellectual and linear attitude toward an experience that is, most typically, emotional and disorderly. The form misdirects us. Argument in this context is unsatisfactory and limited because it simply is inadequate to encompass the complexities of literary experience.

The form of the argument essay, with its demand for a logically proven thesis, also limits the content available for inclusion. Students writing argument essays in response to a particular assignment will each write different essays. Yet the content of those essays will be related: certain material simply won't fit and must be ignored because of the insistence of the form.

Forms are not neutral containers. The argument form, for example, is intolerant of contingency or speculation. It is incapable of the kind of janusian vision demanded by a poststructuralist understanding of the relationships between readers and texts. The form discourages the inclusion and acceptance of contrary points of view.

Privileging the argument form has a devastating impact in the literature classroom. Students learn to expect texts to have single meanings, and teachers see themselves only as skilled textual explicators. These views get in the way of pedagogical success. Students who believe in single textual meanings seriously misunderstand the literary experience. Unwilling to risk being wrong, they are suspicious of their multiple responses. This suspicion is reinforced by teachers who display their own readings (however well-informed) but never reveal their processes or acknowledge the limited nature of any single reading. The argument form serves to increase the craving for certainty in an enterprise where certainty is rarely a legitimate intellectual position.

Increasingly, critical writing is returning to a broader, more exploratory base, and more various forms are being tolerated for its explorations. Narrative, descriptive, and expository developments were displayed, for example, by both Wolfgang Iser (1986) in "The Reading Process: A Phenomenological Approach" and Stanley Fish (1986) in "Interpreting the *Variorum*." Argument was simply incapable of serving their critical purposes.

As we teach students to engage in critical inquiry and critical discourse, we must expand the repertoire of forms we encourage. Instead of limiting ourselves (and our students) to writing argument papers, we follow the model of the professionals in the field and reclaim descriptive, narrative, and poetic discourse for our classrooms. Experience with multiple modes of discourse will release imaginative energies that students will both adapt to more conventional critical forms and employ to create new modes of legitimate critical discourse.

If our first impulse as teachers is to help students become confident, skillful readers, our next must be to teach them to assume a critical stance. A critical stance requires that readers disengage from texts so as that they can act against them. In other words, students must learn how to assert themselves against the voices of the literary canon. The two chapters that follow discuss how to teach students to assume a critical stance obliquely rather than directly, to impose themselves upon literary texts by inflicting their language, their shapes, their thoughts upon the original. The indirect nature of this imposition is freeing. Engaged with texts in this manner, students do not, at first, perceive themselves as being in conflict with the original.

Chapter 6, "Imitating and Transforming Texts," looks at the classical uses of imitation writing and suggests ways in which it can be employed to provide students with an interior view of a text. Students assert themselves against a text by borrowing from it broadly and changing it to suit their own purposes. Chapter 7, "Transforming and Acquiring Texts," is an extension of chapter 6. It, too, takes borrowings from literary texts as the starting points for student writing. However, when students acquire texts, their borrowing is narrower, and their action against the original texts more aggressive. They act to compose creatively and personally rather than critically, and the result is a completely new text that is connected only tangentially with the original.

These two chapters suggest activities that provide students with the imaginative space they need to act critically against texts. The pedagogical aim is to teach students what Peter Elbow calls "wise performance, . . . the ability to engage in contrary behaviors" (1986, 141). Full membership in the literary club depends upon the ability to move aggressively and critically against the privileged status of a traditionally valued canonical text. Reshaping texts to their own purposes, students learn to exercise such critical aggression. In the end, they will be comfortable transferring that experience to the most revered of traditional texts and authors. Freed from literary texts, they will be free to respond critically to them.

6 Imitating and Transforming Texts

Imitation has a long history in teaching both speech and writing. The classical schools of Greek and Roman rhetoric formalized imitation, incorporating it in a pedagogical triad of theory (*ars*), imitation (*imitatio*), and practice (*exercitatio*). Belief in the educational value of imitation was unchanging throughout the Middle Ages and into the Renaissance. In *De Copia*, Erasmus imitated his own message by substituting words, altering word order, and using figurative (instead of literal) language to produce 150 versions of his original "Your letter pleased me greatly."

Although the number of versions Erasmus produced is impressive, he is not unusual in having been inspired to prolific output by imitation. Given a linguistic structure with which to experiment, students, too, enjoy varying bits and pieces of a text repeatedly. One student, working to create an image poem, wrote:

> Cherry red on pale lips
> clutching sticky spoon, a child grins.

She experimented with the image, creating five or six more image poems. Finally, she discovered three that worked together for her and grouped them, calling the poem "Variations":

> Cherry red on pale lips
> clutching sticky spoon, a child grins.
>
> glossy red on pale lips
> within, a girl sobs.
>
> blood red on pale lips
> in a room smothered quiet, a woman dies.

The images continued to intrigue her, and she completed a second poem, again with multiple explorations of the effect of red on an image. Her conscious reference to her earlier piece was evident in her choice of title, "More Variations":

> iodine red on pale lips
> hurt, a child sobs.
>
> glossy red on pale lips
> within, a child sobs.
>
> blood red on pale lips
> in a room smothered quiet, her child sobs.
>
> SHARISE TANAKA

Looking at the two poems together, we can see how the writer imitated her imitations as she experimented with the implications of color in terms of the connotative impact on tone (for example, cherry red clearly doesn't work with "smothered quiet," or "sobs," or "dies").

Many canonized authors explicitly recognized the power of imitation. John Milton's work is thoroughly grounded in imitations of Isocrates, of Latin and Neo-Latin elegies, and of Petrarchan sonnets. Robert Louis Stevenson used imitation to develop his style, aping passages for "some practice in rhythm, in harmony, in construction, and the coordination of parts" and exclaiming, "Like it or not, that is the way to write" (1906, 61). In his *Autobiography*, Benjamin Franklin wrote of his first encounter with Addison and

Steele's *Spectator:* "I thought the writing excellent, and wished... to imitate it" (1985, 124).

In no case did these writers conceive imitation as a sterile, mechanical exercise intended simply to replicate the model. Rather, in each instance, the enterprise was understood to be temporary and generative. Once an imitator has internalized what a model has to offer, a transformation takes place. Milton's *Areopagitica* may be informed by Isocrates, but it uses the original to reconceptualize dramatically the position of an individual in seventeenth-century England. Franklin learned from Addison and Steele by practicing their principles of organization and style but also by taking passages and turning them into verse and back to prose again in order to develop a variety of vocabulary.

Transformation is the key here. It takes only a brief perusal of *Poor Richard's Almanack,* "The Speech of Polly Baker," or "The Sale of the Hessians" to see how Franklin benefited from his efforts, yet we can hardly call these works direct imitations of anything he found in the *Spectator*. Franklin's flexibility and linguistic playfulness generated transformations.

Like Franklin, other receptive practitioners commonly experience unexpected explosions of meaning sparked by the dialectical tensions between the language of the original and that of the imitation. One student created two sentences as she imitated a sentence by Ellington White. The original read:

> Here it was motels and billboards and the hot jangle of neon bursting red over four lanes of concrete (quoted in Brittin and Brittin, 1981).

Her two imitations read:

> Here it was umbrellas and towels and the suffocating heat blanketing the granules of sand.

and

> Here it was calculus books and term papers and the confining rules of behavior boiling up in students.

This movement from a highway setting, to the beach, to a senior's frustration with school in a matter of moments suggests the creative energy unlocked by imitation.

Other students find the same sentence equally generative:

> Here it was total chaos, Nintendo games scattered, toys strewn across the floor, and remnants of food.
>
> Here it was stars and the moon and the cool air of the calm seas over the sandy ground.
>
> Here it was a boy and his dog sitting in the late afternoon heat, and an old fishing pole with a snarled line.

Clearly, imitation expands rather than confines; it generates rather than reduces potential.

Imitation is such a fundamental element of human thinking and learning that we should be able to employ it in our teaching quite naturally. However, somewhere along the way, imitative practice in the classroom has been devalued, sometimes to the point of being equated with copying or plagiarism. For many, imitation and creativity are opposites. Yet, often, imitation is a springboard to creative performance, providing material that an artist shapes to new ends, as in Fielding's *Shamela* or in this delightful student poem in imitation of Wallace Stevens's well-known "Thirteen Ways of Looking at a Blackbird":

> *7 Renditions of a Coconut in D Minor*
>
> 1.
> I always look side-eyed
> At a coconut
> So as not to scare it.
>
> 2.
> I watched with fascination
> The bald, three-eyed Martian.
> His middle eye began to wander.
> Chicken skin crawled up my back.

3.
Floyd ran down the aisle
And released the hairiest bowling ball
I have ever seen.

4.
A shout of jubilation:
Finally after years of innovation,
Thomas Brassiere invented
The ultimate female undergarment
With a coconut.

5.
The sun began to fall.
The barbaric tribe of carrots chanting,
Scalped the unfortunate coconut,
And stuck it on a pole for all to see.

6.
Floyd went out for a pass.
I threw him the ball,
But there was a glare.
Floyd dropped to the ground.

7.
We waited in silence for the enemy.
Suddenly a bomb dropped in front of us.
Men swore their prayers in panic.
The bomb didn't explode.
I looked closer.
Damn, another coconut.

DOUGLAS LUNG

Wallace Stevens's work inspired this poem, to be sure, but only in the most tangential way. Both the content and the humorous tone are the poet's own. The poem must be considered original.

In many classrooms, imitation rarely leads to original performance. The playfulness is absent. Instead of seeing imitation as a process of temporarily dressing up in the costume of another's language in order to explore the implications and excitements of foreign garb, academic emphasis once again centers on the product—both the original model and the imitations produced by students for evaluation.

Furthermore, teachers have focused on using imitation in the classical mode to teach the production of texts—typically, written composition—and neglected its potential to teach literature. Imitation becomes very earnest business, unlikely indeed to produce a *copia* either as rich or as interesting as Erasmus's tour de force or a student's serious experimentation with different shades of red. In addition, when treated rigidly, imitation is equally unlikely to produce any interesting observations regarding the object being imitated. Lacking any personal investment in the exercise, students produce safe, empty responses. More unfortunately, they learn an artificial separation between reading and writing, between literature and composition. They learn to misunderstand the ways in which people make meaning, both as writers and as readers.

Teachers worry about the efficacy of imitation. Model essays, it is argued, can overwhelm students. They are too long and too complex, or perhaps too superior, for students to imitate successfully. Poor students are put in a no-win situation by both teacher and model text; nothing they write can match the standards imposed by the model. Furthermore, imitation does not allow the student to make central rhetorical decisions regarding audience, purpose, and content. Removed from any meaningful context, imitation exercises can degrade into what James Moffett acidly labels "decomposition" (1968, 206–8).

In response to these objections, I would like to suggest three important keys to the successful employment of imitation. First, teachers must maintain an attitude of playfulness. We must encourage adventures with coconuts! Imitation activities provide opportunities for exploration and invention with language; the efforts often amuse, intentionally or not. Taking time to enjoy such amusements, a teacher suggests that manipulating language is an appropriate and creative activity, even though both process and product may well be messy—no potter, after all, ever has clean hands. If we want students to see what they can do with words, they must be free to reconceive, remodel, add, and discard without fear of being thought foolish. An attitude permitting uninhibited experimentation frees students to transform language to serve their own ends and so frees them from overdependence on the originals.

American literature students asked to imitate the form of Jonathan Edwards's well-known sermon, "Sinners in the Hands of an Angry God" seized the opportunity for uninhibited transformation when offered the opportunity to consider "Teachers in the Hands of an Angry Student," "Students in the Hands of an Angry Teacher," or another angry subject. Many began gleefully by imitating the Biblical passage Edwards takes as his text: "Their foot shall slide in due time" (Deut. XXXII. 35). Imitations included the following:

> Shape up or ship out
>
> Boy George: "Do You Really Want to Hurt Me?"
>
> "The Golden Rule: Whoever has the gold makes the rules"
> Arthur Bloch.

The variety of these beginnings suggests the energy students brought to the assignment. In addition, they were able to bring the form of the piece and the rhythm of Edward's language to their writing.

Some students worked to imitate Edwards's use of extended metaphor in addition to taking on the original's rhythm and form. One concluded her piece with a metaphor that feels very typical of Jonathan Edwards:

> The teacher will not save you. To him, you will be a pain in his side, and he will rejoice to be rid of you. A lion wants no more than to have the thorn withdrawn from his paw, rather than to have it driven deeper.

Edwards often uses animal imagery and works to place man-as-sinner in his proper place in a universal hierarchy. To this writer, man is no more than an irritation, a bit of errant vegetable matter gone astray!

Second, what we do with an imitation exercise may be more important to student growth than their original use of the model. Our aim is not for a specific end product but for the insights and discoveries the imitative experience provides. Yet the lessons of imitation assignments are not always transparent to our students. Class discussion increases awareness of the meanings implicit in the dialogue between their imitation and the original; it helps students notice the transformational power of that dialogue and the surprises that emerge from intertextual play. The group can explore the decisions that the model led them to make. I ask students, "What did you add?" to encourage them to identify places where new language penetrates the old. Asking "What did you eliminate?" prompts them to focus on how emphasis can be changed with deletion. Students discuss what the model forces them to ignore, how it defines or limits the shape of their thought. They consider the ways in which form shapes content. They look at how a model enables them to create, how it generates ideas for them.

Several all-purpose questions can serve to propel such discussions. I ask students, "What works?"—both for the model and for their imitations. Wondering what makes a piece compelling, or interesting, or functional helps them identify precisely what generates their responses to literary texts.

Ann Berthoff's question, "How does it change [the] meaning if you put it this way?" (1981, 71–72) is also powerful. Focusing attention on the implications of language choice and meaning, the question makes students more sensitive to language nuances in both the texts they compose as writers and those they interact with as readers. It highlights dramatically how the same idea expressed in different ways is affected, perhaps ever so slightly, by the particular language with which it is expressed.

Stanley Fish's central question—"What does this word, phrase, sentence, paragraph, chapter, novel, play, poem *do?*" (1980, 73)—provides a useful probe with which students can explore the tensions between an original text and their imitations. Asking Fish's question, students confront how their changes necessarily change the original's impact on a reader. Diction and syntax both shape textual response; changes in either reshape that response.

When students explore and explain the differences between original and imitative texts, they simultaneously develop thinking patterns useful for critical inquiry and conscious control of their own powers of linguistic manipulation. Furthermore, imitative practice and the ensuing discussion highlight the interrelationships among texts. Students come to recognize intertextuality as an issue central to the business of critical inquiry. They learn to confront questions of influence: What is an original, and what is a copy? When does a copy distance itself enough from an original to be considered an original itself? What was the original influenced by—what is it a copy of?

Classroom discussion leads to the third key to the successful use of imitation. We need to take advantage of imitation's potential for integrating the processes of critical inquiry—reading, talking, and writing. In combining these three processes, imitation activities force students to replicate three stages typical of critical inquiry: engagement with a text, analytical detachment from the text, and the generation of critical discourse about a text.

Focused attention is a first step in any critical act; imitative writing provides a crucial bridge to the next steps, giving students an opportunity to import alien language—syntax and diction—for their own use. Typically, students can use elements of style and form before they can discuss them. Here are samples written by basic writers experimenting with uncharacteristic language patterns. The original:

> A man on a horse passes slowly, accompanied by a boy on foot who carries a willow branch.
>
> JOAN COLEBROOK, QUOTED IN BRITTIN AND BRITTIN, 1981

The imitations:

> A princess on a horse passes slowly, accompanied by a prince on foot who carries a jeweled staff.
>
> A man in a Mercedes flies by, accompanied by a woman who has a Louis Vuitton handbag.
>
> A boy on a bike passes slowly, accompanied by a retriever who carries a bare stick.
>
> A boy on his skateboard creeps by, alongside a girl on her tricycle, with a broken wheel.

Imitation forces students to add the extra detail that makes an image fresh and concrete. The jeweled staff, Louis Vuitton handbag, bare stick, and broken wheel were practically forced into being by demands of the original sentence structure. Both the writers and their peers identified these sentences as "good writing." As they began to talk about why and how the sentences work, they began to understand similar structures in other passages. In cooperation with an original text, they had tried out stylistic conventions beyond the immediate range of their abilities. Working in cooperation with a text, they incorporated relevant conventions from the original. Soon they would be able to employ them in their own writing.

I now offer several model assignments for you to imitate. Each helps students learn to read like writers. Each provides opportunities for critical conversation. My activities purposely move away from concern only with content, form (including genre and matters of organization and development), and style—the conventional foci of imitative writing, which reflect the assumptions of a product-centered paradigm and block the integration of literature, composition, and critical conversation by removing texts from their rhetorical contexts. Instead, I ask students also to imitate audience and purpose, which focuses critical attention on the living decisions behind every word of a printed text. When these activities suggest a form similar to that of the original text, the writer's attention is deflected from form and centered on an aspect of the rhetorical context considered by the original author. The classifications are meant to suggest the activity's pedagogical focus: when students assume authorial roles, their powers of critical attention are correspondingly heightened.

First, I ask students to create a piece of writing for the same (or a similar) audience as an original. The emphasis, however, is on the relationships between writer and audience and how they influence composing choices made by both students and the original author. Imitation activities that focus on audience help students connect their own experience to those presented by literary texts. Once they have made a personal connection, they are ready for critical evaluation.

ACTIVITY 1

WILLIAM CARLOS WILLIAMS: "THIS IS JUST TO SAY"

Write a poem in which you apologize to someone for doing something, even though you are really not sorry you did it.

Students responding to these directions recognize and replicate the tone of ironic apology with which Williams addresses his audience. They seek to find personal language to describe a temptation as lusciously compelling as Williams's cold plums and work hard to make the shapes of their poems as lean as that of the original. Here are some sample efforts:

This is Just to Say

I am sorry
I knocked you cold,
and your body is sore.

You probably had
your eyes on the ball,
and were planning to score.

Forgive me. You were
such a vulnerable target.
I hope we collide once more!

PAUL CARLTON

I'm Really Sorry Mom

I know you were
late to work
and I really feel bad.

I should have gotten up,
from that warm bed,
heaped with cloudlike covers,
and opened my dream-filled eyes,
earlier.

CHRISTINE TANIGAWA

Excuse Me for Yawning So Big

but it
 just
  came—
   uncontrolled.

I know
 it was rude
  and you're
   embarrassed

but it felt so
 good
  to let it
   all out

arms stretched
 jaw bolted wide.

TESSA YUEN

Students leave this activity with an appreciation for the elegant complexities beneath the smooth surface of Williams's work, an appreciation they are less likely to gain through conventional class discussion alone.

Another imitation activity asks students to assume that they are writing for a specific audience, but here the agendas underlying the writing are more complex.

ACTIVITY 2

■ BENJAMIN FRANKLIN: *THE AUTOBIOGRAPHY*

Pretend you are Benjamin Franklin, writing part of his autobiography to his son William (colonial governor of New Jersey). Create an incident (fictional) that *might* have happened. Choose one that will interest him as well as give him some insight into the kind of man you are. Remember, William may save this document and have it published after your death. How do you want future generations to think of you?

Students responding to these directions confront the implications of dual audience inherent in Franklin's *Autobiography*. Although ostensibly writing for an intimate reader (his son), Franklin had his future reputation in mind as well. Students seeking to address both audiences display an understanding of the effects of Franklin's double agenda. Further, they demonstrate a sensitivity to the language choices in the text as they confront issues of tone that are often opaque to them when they enter a text as apprentice critics.

Other imitation activities direct student attention to a writer's artistic purpose. When such imitations are shared and discussed, the class sees how many different roads reach the same end. They also recognize how particular aesthetic principles function to shape an artistic creation. Students are free to experiment with various forms in this exercise, but most tend to imitate form as well as purpose.

ACTIVITY 3

EZRA POUND: "IN A STATION OF THE METRO"

As defined by Pound, an image is "an intellectual and emotional complex presented in an instant of time." Imagist poetry concentrates on the "image" (the thing itself), uses the language of common speech, and tries for a rhythm like that of a musical phrase. Imagist poets want an image to produce an emotion, to speak for itself. Try to write a poem in which you compress complex thoughts and feelings into a single moment that evokes those thoughts and feelings for a reader.

Here is a poem, written by a student in response to this assignment that taught classmates something important about the ways in which poems can work:

Broken-hearted Lover

The doleful scowl imprinted on his face;
Shattered pieces of glass spattered on the cold floor.

KRISTI DUNG

Both event and emotion are combined in this poem. Classmates quickly appreciated the mimetic form of Kristi's piece and learned to comment on similar strategies in other poems.

Another student poem provided still another lesson. It helped the class see how much meaning could be conveyed using juxtaposition and irony.

A Street in the City

A crisp sheet of newspaper
Dodges.
    Avoiding
Trampling, ignorant feet.

JON KWON

Students in Jon's class were interested in the contrast between the newspaper, a repository of knowledge, and the "ignorant feet" that threaten damage. They also noted the irony implicit in the inanimate object taking conscious action ("Dodges/Avoiding") while the action of the disembodied feet seems so mindless. Once again, imitative writing served to expose enormous complexities beneath the deceptive simplicity of imagist poetry.

This next activity also seeks to highlight the techniques that a writer employs in the service of an artistic principle.

ACTIVITY 4

EDGAR ALLAN POE: "THE FALL OF THE HOUSE OF USHER"

Poe believed that a short story should be written so that every word and event worked to create a single effect. Use the opening paragraph of "The Fall of the House of Usher" as a guide, and write a description that creates a single effect.

Students are usually quick to recognize how Poe piled detail upon detail to create his sullen and melancholy mood. Imitative writing leads students further, as they discover how Poe used sound and the rhythm of his sentences to underlie the gloomy and foreboding scene.

Asking students to imitate the subject matter of a piece produces some especially interesting results and attendant insights. For example, many apprentices come to poetry with a mistaken notion of appropriate subject matter. Imitation writing can help them overcome the initial shock they may feel when first encountering Whitman, Sandburg, or Ginsberg, for example.

ACTIVITY 5

CARL SANDBURG: "CHICAGO"

Choose a city that you like and know well. You should be aware of its flaws as well as its strengths. Write a poem in which you address the criticisms others might make of the city, while expressing your own admiration for it.

Here are the opening lines of a series of imitations of Sandburg's poem. Not surprisingly, many students chose their hometown as these fragments demonstrate:

Honolulu

Business emporium of the islands,
Moneymaker, producer of the people
Player with transportation and the state's tourist industry
Welcoming, bustling, intermingling,
City of the lei greeters.

Honolulu

Paradise of the world
Dream maker, vacation destiny
Peddler of pedicabs and the nation's melting pot.
Sunny, friendly, relaxing:
City of the bronzed bodies.

A more cynical student chose Waikiki as the topic of her poem:

Waikiki

Exploiter of traditional Hawaii
Fake lava rock maker, plastic lei maker,
Weaver of tacky, florescent [sic] Aloha shirts
and signs printed in Japanese.

Sirens, honking, screaming
Made for the tourists:

They tell me you are Paradise, and I wonder,
    Seeing only mountains of concrete.
And they call you the capital of the Aloha state,
    Yet I hear of muggings of visiting foreigners.
And they say your sun is warm and refreshing
    and my reply is: tormented skin peels in agony.
And having seen the truth, I scoff at pamphlets
    advertising "real luau" full of breathtakingly tanned bodies.

AURENE PADILLA

Clearly, Sandburg's poem provided great amounts of creative energy. Students found many other ways, some more distant, of responding. Here are some last examples:

Las Vegas

Tourist trap for the world.
Money maker, uniter of couples,
Players with flashy cars and intimidating limousines,
Bustling, alive, expensive,
"City that never sleeps."

My Room

Junkyard for all teenagers
Mess maker, piles of junk
Place of solitude and comfort
Cluttered, littered, scattered.
room of the lazy occupant.

Activities such as this help students evaluate the aesthetic claim of modern and postmodern art that all experience provides appropriate subject matter for artistic expression.

Theatergoers are intimately conscious of the contributions of stage settings, lighting, and sound to the atmosphere of a production. However, because students lack experience, they rarely recognize the implications of stage directions when they are reading a play. The following activity forces them toward an important critical awareness of the possibilities inherent in stage settings.

ACTIVITY 6

TENNESSEE WILLIAMS: *THE GLASS MENAGERIE*

Choose one of the stage directions in the play and rewrite it, changing the colors of objects mentioned, the lighting, and background sounds. What mood do your changes create? How does the original change? Would your setting be as apt as the original for the action as Williams wrote it?

Some imitation activities ask students to replicate content before they read a particular literary text. These activities are especially useful to students when the content is accessible to them but the form poses potential hazards. The next two activities help students gain access to the opening chapters of novels that begin with interior monologues.

ACTIVITY 7

WILLIAM FAULKNER: *THE SOUND AND THE FURY*

You are mentally retarded. You are outside with somebody named Luster. You can see through a fence to a course where people are playing golf. Luster is looking for a quarter he lost in the grass. Today is your birthday. You are thirty-three years old. Write an interior monologue—a record of your thoughts and feelings. What do you hear? Smell? See? Remember? What can your thoughts show a reader about Luster?

ACTIVITY 8

JAMES JOYCE: *A PORTRAIT OF THE ARTIST AS A YOUNG MAN*

Pretend that you are three or four years old and telling or remembering some things that happened to you. Include the following details: a story about when you met a cow while walking down the road with your father, part of a favorite song, some of the smells of your house, and descriptions of some of your older relatives. Think about the kinds of sentences and words a child might use. How might a child's narration get from one idea to the next?

Here is a student sample in response to the prompt in Activity 8:

> We walk down, down the road, and, and, and horsey—big horsey—say "moo-moo." Oh—cow saying moo. And Daddy picked me up to say hi to the cow, and pet him like a doggie, and he's chewing gum, chewing gum. There's a big hill, big hill—grass and flowers.
>
> "Jack and Jill go up the hill
> To get a pail of water."
>
> Then we went home, back home. Mommy cooking dinner. Uncle and family and grandpa and grandma here. Mommy cooking. Smell like a hamburger. No, not a hamburger. Turkey, yeah, turkey.
>
> Smell aunty's perfume. Aunty smell good, smell pretty. Daddy's pipe stinks! Makes me cough.

I always introduce these two novels in this way. Once students have written for twenty minutes and shared their writing, they are ready to read. Having created such highly personal monologues themselves, they recognize the form and its conventions. When they encounter it as readers, the experience of their imitative writing shows them how to compose meanings from a fragmented, disjointed text. Often, they are astonished at the number of concrete details shared by their work and the original—even though they had no knowledge of the latter until after they did their writing! Instead of finding confusion and anxiety in their initial encounters with Faulkner and Joyce, they read making connections with their own writing and are willing to pursue complexity and partial comprehension.

Asking students to write imitatively treats them as writers and collapses the distance they feel between themselves and a text. They experience the functions and effects of literary structures firsthand. Transforming texts in this way obliquely teaches students to make connections fundamental to literary inquiry and prepares them to participate fully in informed critical discourse.

7 Transforming and Acquiring Texts

In imitative writing, aspects of the original—form, tone, audience, or subject matter, for example—remain recognizably dominant. Even in "7 Renditions of a Coconut," the idea behind the form was Stevens's. However, a reader who *acquires* a text incorporates it in such a way that the text is fitted into his or her identity and loses its autonomous shape; in other words, the reader aggressively asserts self over text and claims the text (or a portion of it) for individual use. Textual acquisition disregards both the original intentions of the author and the original value of the text to the community. The text is reshaped, disfigured even, for new purposes.

Textual acquisition might be classified as misreading or misinterpretation and dismissed as such. Harold Bloom gives us another way to consider it. Strong poets, he suggests, must both respond to their cultural heritage and free themselves of that heritage in order to function both within it and in spite of it. He notes, "Poetic Influence . . . always proceeds by a misreading of the prior poet, an act of creative correction that is actually and necessarily a misinterpretation" (1973, 30). I contend that any critic writing about a text performs a similar "act of creative correction" by imposing his or her language between readers and the work itself. Students need to gain the confidence to perform similar linguistic impositions when they write or talk about texts in a literature class.

Practicing textual acquisition is a necessary and integral component of learning critical inquiry. Activities that engender textual acquisition recognize and insist on misreading and misinterpretation to clear imaginative space within which students as apprentice critics can work. Such activities, however, are not common in our literature classrooms, primarily because of our attitudes toward literary texts. The classroom rituals of both teachers and students reflect our devotion to canonical texts. Reverence is unlikely to accommodate the aggression necessary for full textual acquisition.

We need to free students from textual tyranny. Young, inexperienced, and timid, they feel inadequate to challenge the literary values established by generations of readers. If they dare not trust an unconventional experience with a text, how can they dare to play with the text in any spirit they choose? A full and fair dialectic between critic and text requires equal engagement. Critics must feel themselves equal to both the text and the task to engage in critical discussion. To students, such a sense of equality does not come easily. Feeling unequal, they are able to respond only in ways that are safe and obvious, and their efforts at critical discourse disappoint us.

Donald Murray suggests that readers allow a text "to spark other texts, ghost texts . . . that are born because of the communion between the written text and the experience of the reader" (1986, 244). These "ghost texts," intruding as they do into space occupied by the original, are fundamentally aggressive. New language seeks to displace old. New assertions supersede existing arguments.

Inspired by the pedagogical potential of Murray's ghost texts, this chapter provides sample activities that enable students to spark other texts, to endow their ghost texts with earthly substance. The activities are not particularly revolutionary in form or in content; they are, however, radical in purpose, in the conscious aggression that underpins their design. Each one is designed to liberate the writer to use an original text as a springboard toward something new. Each allows students to experience textual acquisition by consciously developing their ghost texts.

Each of these activities spotlights an aspect of an original text that is then almost immediately diminished by the minimal role it is permitted to play in the resulting discourse. The activities suggest two ways in which students might be led to acquire texts: by acquiring an experience and by acquiring an idea. Other possibilities, however, are multiple; assignments might be designed to help students acquire plot, characterization, or language, for example.

The first sample activity is designed to liberate students from twentieth-century concerns. The activity replicates a common nineteenth-century experience—solitary communion with nature—that came to support an entire philosophical system: transcendentalism. The experience comes after class reading and discussion of selections from Emerson's essays ("Nature," "The American Scholar," "Fate," and "Self-Reliance") and Thoreau's *Walden* and "Civil Disobedience." Not only does this activity provide students with ready material for subsequent writing, but it ensures careful reading and thorough familiarity with the texts being considered.

As the activity begins, students have done a text search to collect passages that appeal to them or express key points made by the authors, and they come to class expecting not an activity, but a unit test. They have been told that the test will be a full period essay and that they will be allowed to use their collected passages when they write their responses.

When the students arrive, I write Thoreau's invitation from *Walden* on the board: "Let us spend one day as deliberately as Nature." I speak briefly about the implications of "deliberately"—careful, thoughtful, reflective, premeditated, intentional, leisurely, or slow in motion or manner. We chat about how nature might be viewed as deliberate. Then I tell them that we are going to accept Thoreau's invitation and "live as deliberately as Nature"—for twenty minutes anyway. They will look at nature, in Emerson's words, through "transparent eyeballs" and allow it to flow freely through them. Instructing them to leave everything behind in the classroom and enjoining them from further communication with one another until we return, I lock the door and lead them to the most secluded outdoor location on the grounds.

Once there, they sit, silently observing whatever comes into view, for twenty minutes. At the end of the time, we return, still silently, to the classroom, and I hand out the following directions:

> "Let us spend one day as deliberately as Nature."
>
> HENRY DAVID THOREAU
>
> From the perspective of the late twentieth century, transcendentalism is a philosophy that needs to be experienced to be understood. Because it is important that it *be* understood—as it is the source of much that is uniquely American—the purpose of the experience of the first part of the period was to give you a taste of transcendental possibilities.
>
> - You read and discussed the philosophies of two major transcendental writers, Emerson and Thoreau.
> - You were asked to isolate yourself as much as possible from communication with other humans.
> - You were given an intensely *individual* exposure to nature.
>
> For the remainder of the period, freewrite on what you learned about nature, yourself, transcendentalism, perceptions of "truth," or reality, or any combination of these topics.
>
> **At Home:**
> Shape the ideas generated during your freewriting into an essay that in some way explores the transcendentalism of Emerson and Thoreau and its relation to you.

Other than giving students a choice of subjects for an essay, the assignment is deliberately vague. As a result, the writing is personal and quite revealing about the quality of each student's individual experience.

As might be expected, many students express initial skepticism about the assignment and its value. One young man wrote:

> When I first read about Emerson's idea to go into the woods and become a transparent eyeball, I thought he was nuts. When I found out that I had to do it for a test, I told myself that this was going to be the worst.

Transcendentalism and its emphasis on observation of nature as a road to universal understanding is likely to seem corny to urban students who often know no natural settings wilder than city parks. Why stare at trees instead of television sets, after all? However, observation apparently convinces students of the importance of Emerson's and Thoreau's values in ways that mere classroom instruction cannot. The same young man finished his essay with the following admission:

> Looking back on that experience now, I think it was pretty awesome. Maybe Emerson really isn't off his block. I learned quite a bit from that twenty minutes.

Many of his classmates learned quite a bit, too.

For some students, the learning is deeply embedded in the emotional aspects of the experience. One student wrote:

> I felt something . . . which took over all my attention and wrapped me entirely in joy, almost reaching ecstasy. I thought of nothing and was aware of no other person. . . . Emerson has remarked that "the lover of nature is he whose inward and outward senses are still truly adjusted to each other" (Nature). My sense was that what I saw with my eyes I felt in my heart and soul.

To a twentieth-century sensibility, this response seems almost gushy; it is easy to dismiss it as adolescent. However, if we read it more generously, we might also note that it is also quite Emersonian. Given an opportunity for reflection and observation, this student experienced the same kind of intellectual and emotional merging that Emerson described in "Nature" when he said, "I have enjoyed a perfect exhilaration. Almost I fear to think how glad I am." Again, engaging in the experience helped this young woman acquire Emerson's text in ways that probably would have been impossible through strictly conventional methods of response. Emerson's words and experience struck a familiar chord to which she was able to respond in kind.

Another student shared Thoreau's pleasure in creating something with his own hands. His emotional satisfaction came as a result of a small invention:

> I picked up a twig and some leaves and began fiddling around.... Absentmindedly, I fastened a leaf to a twig. I connected another twig to the other end of the leaf. Then to the second twig, I attached a round leaf to act as a cup. Presto! I had created my very own wind meter that could point out the direction the wind was blowing.

He, too, was released by the experience into an Emersonian expression of emotion. He wrote that a "gush of pride and accomplishment overwhelm[ed]" him because of his creation. He had built something tangible, and he knew how it worked. He expressed confidence that he could "repair it when necessary." He felt a sense of connection with Thoreau; not only had he used his ingenuity to build something of practical value, but he could understand the emotional satisfactions central to such construction. The final line of his essay reveals his sense of pleasure at both creation and connection: "This 'shared' experience could never have been found in a store nor bought for a price. It was all mine!"

For other students, the exercise provides an opportunity to reflect upon processes of perception and learning. One young woman expressed annoyance with her earlier lack of awareness:

> I've lived... for seventeen years and only recently have I discovered what grass really looks like. I've stepped on grass, sat on grass, and lain on grass many times during my existence... yet it took me seventeen years to discover that grass grows in clusters and not in single strands. What's wrong with me? Why haven't I noticed this before?

Lessons in perception have enormous potential as we work to teach critical consciousness. We can suggest to students that learning about grass or insects or trees and learning about poems or essays or novels require similarly focused attention. We can remind them that returning to look at familiar landscapes often rewards us with glimpses of previously unnoticed details.

A second young woman told how her vision of the world changed and how her newly raised consciousness set her apart from those around her:

> After my twenty minute escape to some "Walden Pond" outside the busy parameters of school, I, too, felt a bit more knowledgeable about

> the world around me. As I moseyed down to my period five class I felt the warmth of the sun hugging me... and I felt a soft and patient pity for the others who bustled and dashed past me, ignoring a light, passing breeze, the clear soft sky, and the shrubs that nodded along the rough cement path.

Daily pressures blocked her classmates' pleasure in the natural world; sensitivity to her new vision made her conscious of their blindness. Such enhanced awareness of recent blindness is often exactly what inspires a critic, enabling the literary enrichment of others.

Another student was surprised to find how much was going on in the tiny area he had blocked out for observation. First, he replicated Thoreau's experience and watched "a pair of ants who were locked in combat... as [they] struggled on top of a brick." However, soon his attention was forced elsewhere: "So intently was I watching [the ants] that I didn't notice the grey bug that had crawled onto a brick only a foot from the ants." He was surprised that he had "missed so much of the action going on" and came to understand that

> the small area before me was a vast area whose entire landscape I could never observe all at once.

His experience with the insects paralleled that of a reader with a text. Our attention is deflected, and we miss parts; given a reader's subjective processes of composing texts, nobody, after all, can hope to notice everything.

A fourth student had this to say about the relationships between observation and learning:

> Observation, although a major factor in learning, can't teach you everything. There are some things which can only be learned through reason and experience. By reasoning, one... becomes more perceptive because in trying to come up with an answer, one must first look for a clue. In other words, one can only come up with an answer after he has enough things to base his judgment on.

Observation is central to learning but only useful insofar as the observer can create an intellectual framework within which to evaluate perception.

The thoughtful level of response generated by a twenty-minute experience is impressive. Students grapple with their observations and make applications, many of which have direct impact on their developing critical abilities. As they learn to observe and reflect on their observations, they experience close readings of the natural texts provided by the outdoors and move to critical evaluations of their readings. Later, they transfer this same movement to their readings of literary texts.

These essays reveal the philosophical, questioning attitude central to all critical inquiry. One student, for example, assumed the posture of Emerson's "Man Thinking" and explored the notion of reality, a concept whose abstraction typically provides a dangerous quagmire for even the seasoned philosopher. He was able, however, to thread a way through the conceptual dangers and reached an understanding reminiscent of Aristotle's well-known commentary on a bell sounding in a wood empty of ears:

> I heard many birds singing, but I could not see them. Therefore, it was not apparent to me that they existed. Again, to a child who has never made the connection between a chirp he has heard and the feathered creature we know as a bird, the sound does not indicate that a bird actually exists. In the child's mind, the bird does not exist, there is only the sound which he hears. Likewise, as I assumed the role of Man Thinking, the bird did not exist in my mind and henceforth did not exist for me. There was only sound.

Epistemological excursions like these are rarely possible when we restrict students to conventional responses to literary texts, and yet such excursions reveal precisely the kind of thinking we wish them to experience—critical and creative, analytical and generative.

A second student philosopher found a "new appreciation of everything" he saw and expressed his happiness to be alive before he asked himself, "Is it important that everything exists?" At first, he feared that he was asking a "stupid question" but pushed on nevertheless:

> I started to hypothesize what the situation would be like if nothing existed. I visualized blackness and . . . and that was it [his ellipses]. Who would care if everything did not exist? There wouldn't be anyone or anything to care about anyway.

He continued by hypothesizing that God "would care" but noted that "giving God anthropomorphic qualities is purely hypothetical. . . ." He continued, "We only live by standards we create for ourselves." Following his line of reasoning further, he observed that death is what makes life meaningful and wondered, "I want to know what makes life more significant than lifelessness?" He went on to note:

> How do we know that the standards we live by are correct? If we question these aspects of existence, then everything is questionable.

With no training in philosophy, this student moved from transcendentalism to existentialism. The original, nineteenth-century texts coupled with his experience to propel him, via critical inquiry, into twentieth-century philosophy.

These students assimilated Emerson's and Thoreau's essays in individual ways. They *acquired* them by incorporation, and the personal experience of each student emerged as the central focus of reflection and discussion. Frequent gestures to passages from Thoreau and Emerson, however, and comments on feelings of connection suggest that, rather than being tangential and solipsistic, the students' discourse was consciously referential. A triangular relationship occurred among student, experience, and literary text(s) that appeared to provide students with an opportunity first to engage both text and experience and then to disengage for a reflective process, both creative and critical. Because of personal assimilation—textual acquisition—these students became equal participants in critical relationships with the text(s).

A teacher's task is to receive such essays in ways that help students examine their observations and critical behaviors. This is easier than it may seem. Either through group discussion or in individual conferences, teachers can lead students to approach their essays as they would approach literary texts. Students learn to notice their observations and the connections they made to the original, and the implications of both. They can look at the ways in which Emerson's and Thoreau's texts influenced their own thinking. After they become aware of their critical behaviors, students can make productive transfers when they are required to act conventionally as literary critics.

A second activity that helps students acquire texts for themselves focuses on the incorporation of a specific idea from an original into a student text. This assignment functions well with works that are particularly quotable. Shakespearean plays, for example, contain an abundance of aphorisms that are easily isolated for student use. The work of Alexander Pope similarly provides ample opportunities for student acquisition. But, to continue in the transcendental spirit with which the discussion in this chapter began, the examples I offer here are based on passages from Emerson. The activity is as follows:

- Find a brief passage from Emerson that states a general doctrine or "truth" that appeals to you. Write a poem that incorporates Emerson's words in some way.

Some might question the validity of a poem as a mode of response to an essay, but willingness to approach one genre with another is central to textual acquisition. The goal of the activity is explicitly to dislocate texts and forms in order to relocate them for personal use. Narrative, descriptive, or poetic discourse often generates richer insight than does logical examination. The activity encourages students to be aggressive in textual acquisition simply because a poem is not a conventional critical form. Furthermore, writing poems enables them to experiment with a form that is often underused.

Asking students to write stories also works. I find that when students are asked to write stories (instead of poems) to illustrate a passage, they tend to respond with fables, adding the passage after the narrative ending. The wise sayings from Poor Richard have provided my students with inspiration for many interesting narratives.

Activities intended to encourage textual acquisition must be designed to tolerate a range of highly idiosyncratic responses. Both topic and student text emerge from the creative interaction between the literary text and the student's prior knowledge. The vagueness of these instructions is, therefore, intentional. Students are given little direction in choosing a passage and no direction regarding the shape of their poems. Openness is central to successful acquisition; this activity gives students space in which to move because it does not prescribe any one, appropriate response.

Several examples illustrate the variety of form, subject, and tone with which students respond to this activity. More interestingly, the examples also display a broad range of critical observation. It should be noted at the outset that these are the aspects of the assignment that are interesting pedagogically. No effort has been made to help students act as strong poets. The poems are viewed in terms of the thinking they reveal rather than measured against an aesthetic standard.

One student began with Emerson's warning that "imitation is suicide" ("Self-Reliance"):

> Imitation is suicide;
> We must never copy,
> Or else we will conform
> And our brains get loose and floppy.

The language is clearly the student's, and yet it nicely echoes Emerson's warning against the dangers of conformity. The poet's image of students with brains that are "loose and floppy," moreover, suggests the very distinction that Emerson made in "The American Scholar" between "a mere thinker" and "Man Thinking." Textual acquisition enabled this synthesis.

The student continued to explore the pressures to conform imbedded in his educational experience. "We must use our own ideas/ And follow through with them," he wrote, but many courses "don't stimulate thought." Education is experienced as "study from books," and students are not encouraged to find or use a "fresh idea." The student caustically concluded:

School doesn't help you;
It pounds information in with a girder.
If imitation is suicide,
School is pure murder.

Emerson's words coupled with the opportunity for creative engagement, and this student was able to recognize the truth in Emerson's message. This recognition became the first step toward the critical distance he needed to observe the gap between Emerson's ideal and his own experience.

A second student connected Emerson's language with childhood experience. Her poem, "The Artist," begins with a description of a youngster assembling the tools for her creative activity—a shovel and a pail—and choosing a quiet location for her work. When she commences

Shaping and sculpting
With an expert's skill,
Trained eye and nimble hands
Are careful with detail.

After "days of practice," she feels she has attained "perfection" and created "the masterpiece." Her pride is evident. Her work is

One of a kind
Unique and quite rare
A display for the world
to admire and adore.

Her pleasure with her creation is short-lived, as an adult voice intrudes:

"Honey how sweet!
Is that mud pie for me?"

Her carefully constructed "masterpiece" is seen as casual and unformed, and the poem concludes wistfully with Emerson's adage from "Self-Reliance": "To be great/ Is to be misunderstood. . . ."

Another student also turned to observations of her childhood as she considered Emerson's comment in "Nature" that "The sun illuminates only the eye of the man, but shines into the eye and heart of the child." She used an open form for her poem.

The Magic in a Child's Eye

When I was
five,
the sun
gave me
tender warmth
as I
romped
in the lush
grass.
Birds sang
joyful melodies
and rainbows
glowed in glory.

Now, I'm
older
and the sun
is but
another star
and the green grass
is chlorophyll.
Birds make
noise
because of their
body structure
and rainbows are
refractions
of light.

As we get
older,
the Magic
grows
dimmer.
Truly

"the sun
shines
into the heart
of the child"
and
"illuminates
only the eye
of the man."

Magic touches the heart of a child, and sadly enough fails the heart of the adult.

Students display a wide range of content, form, and critical comment in response to this assignment. One student wrote a Shakespearean sonnet exploring Emerson's assertion that Fate is that which limits us. She suggested that, if Emerson is right, redefinition of our limits might enable us to overcome fate. Another likened Emerson's "mere thinker" to a mirror: "Placed in front of a white wall,/ It shows nothing but white." He noted: "A mere thinker like a mirror,/ Only imitates," and is incapable of creating anything original. Few students chose the same passages. Even those that did found very different ways in which to respond. Individual variation expanded the learning possibilities for the group as a whole.

Acquiring texts allows students to be original thinkers rather than just mirrors. The activities presented in this chapter help students decide meaning, rather than mirror the meanings of others, because they lead students to explore texts imaginatively and creatively and, in doing so, to acquire them. The critical (and pedagogical) value of textual acquisition centers in the ways in which it insists on synthesis. Synthesis—of text, context, and critic—is key to critical discourse.

CONCLUSION

As noted earlier, our teaching of critical reading and writing is shaped by assumptions about texts and interpretation and by conventions of critical form that are pedagogically and epistemologically suspect. Texts do not have single determinate meanings. Reading is not a matter of passive reception of language from a page. Argument is neither the best, nor the only, useful form for critical discourse.

We should not be surprised that our critical activities are so patterned (often unconsciously). We can only see the world through the conventional lenses of our own education and experience as literature teachers/practicing critical inquirers. Imbedded in our particular critical communities (our training, our departments), we find it difficult to detach and examine our methods of performance.

Yet we must. Our conventional methods are limiting. They prevent adequate examination of texts. They misrepresent the nature of critical discourse outside the classroom. They lead us to base our teaching on an artificial and fundamentally dysfunctional model.

Dialogue journals, process logs, and reading responses direct students to repeated, recursive explorations of texts. The activities presented in these last two chapters seek to overcome some limitations of the argument form by providing alternatives for classroom use. We are offering students experiences and enlarged ways of seeing. We are freeing them from the tyranny of canonized texts and providing alternative forms for critical response during their apprenticeship.

Providing alternatives—these and others—is crucial. Students need to be able to think in terms other than hierarchy and authority. Hierarchy and authority place critics in a competitive position both with texts and with other critics. The tendency is to claim supremacy of one critical view over another. This leads to the assertion of single (and therefore fundamentally incomplete) readings. In the classroom, claims of mastery block collaboration and discussion and close down interpretations where we want students to open up their readings.

Choice among forms is legitimate. When teachers choose forms for student writing, we must do so with a clear understanding of their particular values and limitations. When we define forms for students, even when we do so in the most generous terms (as in "write an essay" or "write a poem"), we should do so for pedagogical reasons, not because we feel that one form is inherently better than another. Furthermore, when we choose forms for student writers, we need to be conscious of the artificiality of our determination and aware that one of our eventual objectives is to lead students to make such choices independently.

The writing activities in this section teach students ways to connect with texts, transforming and acquiring them for new ends. Transforming reduces the distance between students and texts via processes of personal and active engagement; as students act upon texts to change them, the texts reveal openings for interpretation that were previously unavailable.

Imitative and acquisitive transformations are powered by imagination. Imitation writing requires a student to imagine a new audience, purpose, and subsequent content for an existing text. When students acquire texts, they imaginatively link themselves with other authors and their writing. Approaching texts imaginatively instead of analytically frees students from the conventional tyrannies that often block their ability to read and write critically.

Imaginative writing activities lead students to develop an aesthetic response to artistic creation. They are an excellent way to help students gain an appreciation of both product (literary form) and process (creative artistry). Creative alignment with texts provides students with interior views of the literature they examine. They live its ideas, experiment with its language, and explore its possibilities. Interiority generates both appreciation and a confidence that otherwise often eludes inexperienced readers.

My experience is that the writing normally relegated to the creative writing class, when coupled with literary study, works to improve students' expository writing. In addition, imaginative writing assignments serve to improve students' reading. Operating creatively as writers and readers, they begin to transfer the structure and technique for one process to the other, often unconsciously.

Sadly, literature classrooms typically separate critical and creative endeavors. While we may ask students to write short stories and poems, we fail to knit those writing activities into the patterns of critical inquiry that are the object of our efforts. Instead, they are considered marginal writings; we squeeze them in among assignments that we consider more important and eliminate them when pressured by limited time. Yet, as the writing activities in this section have demonstrated, creative forms have the power to release a wealth of critical thought.

We cannot afford to ignore creative thinking during analytical tasks, just as we cannot ignore analytical thinking while creatively composing. If we regularly dismiss the unusual, the nonlinear, or the intuitive when we solve problems, these fertile intrusions become less and less conscious. If we ignore random thoughts rather than examining them for possible value, we limit our potential for creative critical thinking, and we doom ourselves—and our students—to a limbo of the ordinary and the conventional.

We have come far as we seek to expand habits of literary study—of the critical composing of readers and writers. We now envision students using writing to explore their knowledge of literary texts. We recognize the emergence of their critical insights as they manipulate texts, transforming them for other uses.

SEQUENCING CRITICAL INQUIRY

INTRODUCTION

Stand-alone assignments—those with little or no connection to previous or future activities in a course—are practically useless to both student and teacher, no matter how much fun they may seem and no matter how much students may claim to like them. Stand-alone assignments indicate a grab-bag approach to teaching—grab anything interesting that will keep the kids quiet on Monday morning or Friday afternoon. They reflect a lack of planning that is unprofessional and unproductive.

Education, in the full sense of the word, suggests long-term growth and permanent, readily accessible increments to a learner's store of information. Learners who are truly educated develop experientially as they use information in repeated and various contexts. Education is a repetitive and recursive process by which discrete moments of experience must be connected by the curriculum, the teacher, and, ultimately, by the student, if they are to have impact.

The chapters in this section present models for sequencing activities that help students experience critical inquiry and lead them to write conventionally formal critical essays about literary texts. The sequences encourage a process that moves from personal and expressive writing (journals, logs, freewritings, poems) through discussions of student writing and the texts upon which it is based, to analytical writing (essays, arguments, reviews).

The power of sequential activities lies in the way they make complex tasks accessible to average students. These activities recognize students as critical apprentices and provide opportunities for exploration and practice. Students successfully complete tasks that would have been beyond them if undertaken independently or in isolation. Repeated sequencing throughout apprenticeship encourages the assimilation of critical behaviors that allows students to function independently. From a pedagogical point of view, the processes in which students engage during these activities are as important as the individual products they produce.

In these sequences, students experience movement from the interior to the exterior in two ways: (1) as readers, they move into texts, making personal connections as they experience them, before moving to a critical-analytical distance; and (2) as composers, they move from creating their own critical discourse to assuming roles as receivers of similar discourse.

Designed for beginners to critical inquiry, the two sequences that follow concentrate on providing practice with contextually grounded (and intertextually aware) comparison and analysis. Once students are comfortable with this, other critical strategies become available. Several are discussed in the conclusion to this section.

In the first sequence model, student writing deals with relationships between one of Hawthorne's short stories and his *Scarlet Letter*. In the second, student papers are on poems by Emily Dickinson. The sequences suggested are not content specific; that is, the Hawthorne paper might have used a series of activities similar to the one described for the Dickinson paper or vice versa. Both sequences or modifications of either can be productively used with other texts.

Activities and their order may vary within sequences, but each sequence is designed according to several basic principles:

1. The sequence begins by establishing a context: historical, cultural, or biographical. Contextual activities become opportunities for students to develop research skills and to practice using bibliographical form.

2. Each sequence introduces, provides practice with, and helps to refine some general critical principles. For example, in the

first sequence, the entire class works on symbolism, ambiguity, Hawthorne's interest in guilt and sin, and using quoted material effectively. The next sequence addresses strategies for reading poems, Dickinson's characteristic themes and stylistic techniques, and the notion of near or slant rhyme, as well as techniques for peer response and summary writing. Commonly, the general principles are a combination of things specific to an author (or a historical period, or a form) and things general to critical composition (oral or written).

3. Students often work independently on an activity that parallels the inquiries in which they are engaged during class.

4. Small groups—pairs or larger—provide timely feedback at key stages in the independent project.

5. After extensive peer feedback to a draft, students have an opportunity to revise before publication and group comment.

6. The audience for the papers is (at a minimum) an entire class. Papers can be typed on dittos or mimeographed (by students!), photocopied, passed around, or read aloud, but they must not be directed solely to the teacher, or the project fails. When teaching more than one section of a course, I cross-fertilize, giving each class an opportunity to read papers from the other group. Students writing on the same topics are especially interested in each other's work, and I ask them to write responses to one another's papers.

Consistent application of these principles assures that students have multiple opportunities to explore texts, to receive feedback on the validity of their observations, and—collaboratively—to develop some principles of evaluation: for an author, a genre, a period, or a work.

The principles also help provide a literary experience with texts that approximates the typical modus operandi of skilled practitioners: engagement, observation, discussion with peers, refinement of evaluations, public commitment to particular readings, and widespread discussion of those readings. Students must learn about specific texts, of course, but, more broadly, they must learn how to operate as members of a critical community.

The sequences are intended to be suggestive rather than prescriptive. Included with descriptions of the activities are comments regarding design, reason for inclusion, and considerations of order. Such comments should help other teachers adapt and transfer similar sequences to their own classrooms. Any absolute sequence is impossible. Sequence design depends upon the needs and abilities of the students in relation to the difficulty of the text, the course emphasis and objectives, and a sequence's relation to other sequences.

It is tempting to think of teaching critical development in hierarchical terms, beginning with easy tasks to develop elementary skills and moving to hard tasks to develop sophisticated abilities. However, learning a new task is more recursive than linear. Each forward movement may be followed by a recursive move back to an earlier stage (or stages) when a difficulty is encountered. For example, a person using a new recipe may read the instructions several times, before beginning to work with ingredients. In the course of preparation, the cook may return to the directions for validation or redirection. These recursive moves increase the operator's familiarity with information before (or while) manipulating it. Faced with a familiar task, on the other hand, an operator begins elsewhere. An experienced cook often begins with application (preparation of the dish) and jumps to evaluation ("this doesn't taste as good as last time") before moving back to knowledge ("too much salt spoils the flavor").

Different projects, undertaken for different reasons, demand different forms of engagement. Different levels of experience and prior knowledge are demanded by each project. We must provide students with many kinds of textual engagement. They do not progress from worse to better, or from easy texts to difficult ones, as much as they develop from less experienced to more experienced readers.

Frank Smith notes that "being unable to think about something in a particular manner indicates unfamiliarity with the subject matter rather than an underlying inadequacy of thought itself" (1988, 48). Lack of experience, not difficulty of cognitive operation, prevents informed critical operation. If we wish students to demonstrate their ability to think, write, and talk critically about texts repeatedly and independently, we must design ways for them to do so successfully. Our task is to open up the literary experience for students, to create sequences of activities that enable successful interactions with texts and successful critical distancing.

Our sequences should be recursive, returning students again and again to engagement with the text, engagement with their response to the text, and engagement with each other. We should think of our sequences as webbed rather than linked end to end. We are not stringing beads on a thread but weaving a fabric. We are not teaching authors (or their novels, short stories, and poems) but the relationships among them and among their many readers. Critical inquiry demands connection.

Interwoven activity sequences that combine reading, writing, and discussion help students experience a text in itself and in context—in terms of relationships within and among texts and times and within the discourse community discussing those relationships. Such sequences also provide students practice with critical action. Frequent feedback develops the confidence and skill they need for full participation in critical conversations.

8 Sequencing Inquiry into Fiction

Many literature courses bear an unfortunate resemblance to Thanksgiving dinner. We create banquets, literary feasts spread out in historical sequences or generic groupings (either by theme or by form). We stuff students' minds with spoonfuls of this and slices of that until flavors and textures merge into uncomfortable heaviness, and students yearn for naps.

They learn more from a simpler menu, one that provides extended exposure, not nibbles. We want to teach students both to experience and to evaluate literature. Yet course design often neglects the adequate context students need to make literary observations and judgments. They will gain more from in-depth looks at an author, period, or genre because they develop a sense of the context of individual works. By reading several works by a single author, students begin to recognize issues that repeatedly interest the writer. A single Hawthorne novel or story does not expose the author's recurring interest in guilt and the power of sin; each narrative seems highly individual because of the skill of the storyteller. Thus, the scope of a reader's observations of one text made without the benefit of knowing the others is limited.

Students also need opportunities to explore a range of possibilities within a particular form. Readings of a Shakespearean sonnet are enriched by experiences with sonnets by Wyatt or Spenser or Milton or Rossetti. Understanding of Shakespeare's use of the form is expanded by exposure to modern practitioners like Edna St. Vincent Millay or W. H. Auden.

I designed the following sequence for classes of high-school juniors studying American literature. It comes within the first month of the course, at a point when students have already established a context in which to work. They have read at least three of Nathaniel Hawthorne's short stories—usually "Young Goodman Brown," "The Minister's Black Veil," and "Rappaccini's Daughter." They have read *The Scarlet Letter.* Sometimes, they have viewed the 1979 WGBH film version of the novel. They have read about Hawthorne and his life. They know about Puritans and Hawthorne's relationship to them (one of his uncles was a judge in the Salem witchcraft trials). They have talked about symbolism, allegory, ambiguity, irony, and paradox. They have examined Hawthorne's interest in moral problems—evil, sin, and guilt—and in the relationship between the individual and society. They are ready for a project that will synthesize what they know. Having offered students a rich informational context, I now want to provide the collaborative context in which they can operate critically.

This particular sequence leads students to an expository essay—an essay of critical exploration. I have several objectives for the sequence:

1. To give students practice in collaborative critical inquiry.
2. To help students make new (that is, not previously discussed in class) connections among several of Hawthorne's works.
3. To give students practice using direct quotations properly and effectively.
4. To wean students from the habit of writing linear essays in which they make and develop only a single point.
5. To evaluate students' knowledge of the literature.

This writing assignment does multiple duty. We spend so much time discussing and exploring the texts, both before and during the sequenced activities, that the students become quite familiar with the literature. The assignment also extends students' mechanical abilities (I use it to teach conventional use of quotations and ellipses, for example) and provides experience with collaborative language use. At the same time, it assesses individual performance; I use the essays to evaluate my students' knowledge of Hawthorne, their ability to select and use quoted material, and their performance as literary critics. I ask: Do they know the material? Can they use it? Can they offer the group useful and insightful observations and interpretations?

The sequence might be thought of as spiral in shape. It repeatedly twists students into a textual experience and then out to acknowledge responses; it turns them inside for personal responses and outside for communal discussion; it moves them into expressive writing and out to transactional discussion and writing. The sequence ends, as do all such sequences in my classes, with publication. Each student shares his or her work with a group, sometimes orally, sometimes by providing copies of the finished piece. Student texts become part of the critical context of the inquiry community.

The sequence begins with the following directions:

HAWTHORNE PAPER

You will be writing an expository essay in which you explore one of the following topics in *The Scarlet Letter* and at least one of Hawthorne's short stories:

- Hawthorne's use of a central symbol.
- The effect of guilt.
- The nature of evil.
- Hawthorne's use of fantasy.
- Hawthorne's use of landscape.
- The role of women.

Tonight, spend twenty minutes freewriting (start writing and keep writing) about your chosen topic. Remember you are talking to yourself on paper. Don't be concerned about false starts or "dumb ideas." Just keep writing steadily, and try to get as much down as you can. Most of you will have several pages of writing by the end of twenty minutes. Your ideas will be shared.

While I am tempted to elaborate on the topics ("How are women treated in Hawthorne's fictions? What role(s) do they play? How might you characterize the relationships between men and women?"), I have learned not to. Students need to generate such questions for themselves. Too often, extra directions close down a subject for uncertain writers. I want the timid ones to feel free to open up.

Before students leave class, they make their topic choices. This sequence is most effective when at least three students work on the same topic. Sometimes, a topic is not chosen. Sometimes, topics are combined or modified (becoming "the symbolism of evil" or "guilt and relationships between men and women," for example). That is fine. Topic distribution can reflect student interest and the demands of group size as long as students work to have groups of at least three. The key is to have groups whose members are exploring the same topic.

At the next class meeting, students read over their freewriting and mark passages or ideas that seem promising. I use this time to check progress and give comfort or advice. When students have finished marking their passages, I have each one create an inquiry list of all the questions about the topic that he or she can generate. While I might model one or two ("Are sin and evil the same thing?" "How does Hawthorne define each?"), the burden of question formation properly rests with the students. The next step is for them to share their questions with their groups and to expand their inquiry lists to encompass questions from the others.

Students then return to the text for a closer look. T. S. Eliot reminds us that "it is difficult to make the facts generalize themselves" (1964, 123–24). Students who are inexperienced in critical inquiry frequently fail to have facts in hand when they first think about a subject; instead, they tend to define a thesis, plan the paper, and only then look for quotations to fill out the discussion. A text search forces them to restructure that pattern of behavior.

HAWTHORNE PAPER

Text Search

Keeping your inquiry list and your freewriting ideas in mind, scan the novel and the story(ies) you have chosen for passages that seem pertinent to

> your topic. Your job is to be a collector, and you want your collection to be as complete as possible. Don't worry if you are unsure about how something fits.
>
> Writing on only the *left*-hand page in your notebooks, make a list of all the quotations you find. Skip several lines between each quotation. Be sure to record page numbers so you can find the passage again. You may wish to abbreviate titles (*SL*, for example).
>
> We will be working with these lists in our next class.

Asking students to write out all the quotations they find helps circumvent the tendency of beginning writers to use much longer passages than are needed to illustrate a point. If students are unfamiliar with the conventions of using ellipses, this is a useful time to teach them.

Although a text search is time-consuming, students quickly recognize its value. Evaluating this portion of the sequence, one student wrote:

> My ideas were enriched by the text search because as I was looking for specific things . . . I glanced over other things that I never would have thought of.

Another agreed, noting that the text search told her which ideas

> had a strong case that I could support richly from the text. Instead of just deciding on one idea . . . I could see all my ideas and the various quotes and decide which topic would be the best for me.

The text search also increases familiarity with a text's details and consequently increases the range of potential action. Another student indicated how important those details can become:

> The text search helped to solidify some of the ideas that I already developed, but more importantly the search brought out some fine details that led me to some new ideas—one of which eventually became the focus of my paper.

Clearly, this student was able "to make the facts generalize themselves" in a useful way.

When students bring the results of their searches to class, I ask them to treat the quotations as the first part of a dialogue journal, taking the place of individual observations, comments, or collectings. Now they are to spend twenty minutes using the facing pages to comment on their quotations. Keeping the topic of inquiry in mind, they note and comment on recurring images, language, and other patterns.

They are now ready to move into their groups with the following directions:

HAWTHORNE PAPER

Group Discussion—Directions

1. Check to see that you are all working on the same topic.

2. Check to see that everyone is prepared with the first freewriting, the inquiry list, and the text search (commented upon).

3. As a group, discuss your topic, your ideas, and the evidence you have found. Take notes as you discover ideas that are new to you.

4. When the group feels it has fully explored the topic, it should disband. If there is time left in the period, you may begin on the following assignment:

Assignment

Now it is time for a leisurely chat with yourself about your topic and what you want to do with it. Take a few moments to review all the material you have collected so far: your first freewriting (marked), your inquiry list, your text search (commented upon), and your notes from class discussion. When you have reread everything carefully, freewrite for twenty-five to thirty-five minutes, trying to seek a *center,* an *inquiry question,* for your paper. If you already have a center, use your writing to consider how you will shape your inquiry question. What issues will you consider? What terms will you need to define? What relationships are central to your discussion?

When you have finished freewriting, try to write a *centering sentence* (or more) that expresses the focus and direction you think your paper might pursue. These sentences may become part of your introduction.

While peer response to paper drafts has become accepted practice, group discussion as a prewriting activity within the context of a traditional literature class is less common. Teachers are reluctant to use groups in this way because of concerns about plagiarism and an insistence that student work should result from original effort. Such insistence assumes that assistance in identifying appropriate ideas to include in papers is cheating. Pedagogical design is shaped by a moral consideration rather than an educational one.

Unfortunately so. This is, after all, a learning situation. Students are practicing. Talking complements writing. Groups serve as resources for their members, providing all with a wider range of information than any member has available alone. Group discussion furnishes ideas but also exposes how ideas form, giving group members an opportunity to use similar thought processes. Groups help students acquire the confidence and independence that add force to a writer's voice and enable movement beyond safe, often boring, responses to work that is truly insightful. Finally (and ironically), one of the main benefits of group discussion is that it makes learners more independent (Abercrombie 1960).

Opportunity for group talk is particularly valuable before students begin to draft papers because it helps them expand their web of understanding. Student topics and developmental directions evolve from interactions between the text and each reader's prior knowledge. This expanded web, this richer base of prior knowledge, enables the generation of new ideas. An opportunity to discuss subjects enlarges the potential for critical comment when students begin to write. A research project I designed around an activity sequence similar to the one described here revealed a great deal of content in student papers (25 percent of the ideas in the group studied) emerged invisibly between group discussion and drafting. Evidently, the group provided an arena for rehearsal and the clarification of information. Students left their groups feeling confident about their projects and knowing what they needed to do to make them successful.

When students return to class with their second freewriting and their centering sentences, group members help them with clarifications and necessary revisions. By now, students are armed with content. They have plenty to say, and their centering sentences have given them a sense of how to control or limit their content. But they need ways to shape their papers; with such a rich lode of content to mine, they are unsure where to dig first or how to display

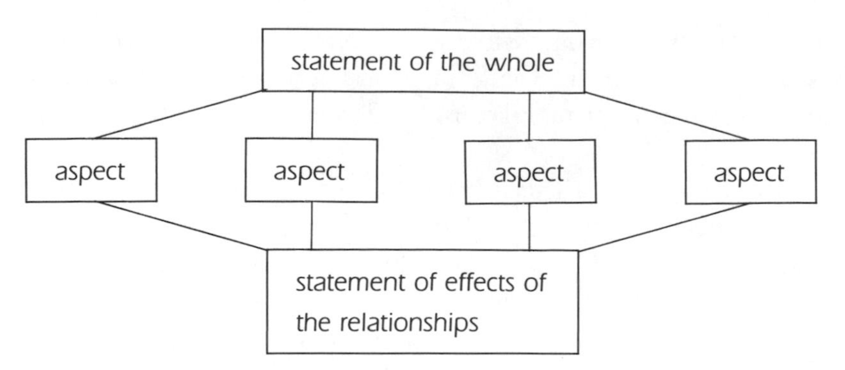

Figure 8–1 Part to Whole

their treasure. The linear form of the thesis-driven essay with which they are most familiar is inadequate for the complexity of this particular task. Yet it is so ingrained that students find it difficult to abandon.

We could easily provide students with nonlinear models. For example, if we are asking them to write an essay of analysis in which their task is to see how the different parts of a text work together, we might illustrate the relationships with a diagram like the one in Figure 8–1. Providing alternative diagrams, however, simply replaces one visual model with others and does nothing to address the underlying weakness inherent in all generic shapes: discourse form is dependent upon, and interwoven with, discourse content. Considerations of one must necessarily involve considerations of the other. Students do not need artificially constructed forms; instead, they require ways to envision the organic relationship between content and form. They need a strategy to create the unique shapes demanded by each writing task. They need a technique that is infinitely flexible, simple to revise, and easy to do. They need to learn card diagramming.

In preparation for card diagramming, students write their main points on individual 3-by-5 cards or slips of paper. These main points may be sentences (if they are assertions, perhaps) or phrases (if they indicate an area of discussion, such as "woman as a nurse"). For example, a list of points generated by an examination of the role of women in "The Minister's Black Veil" and *The Scarlet Letter* might include the following:

- forced isolation
- they provide social commentary
- express views of community
- dependent upon male decisions
- act as nurses
- provide comfort at time of (male) death
- stand up for needs, beliefs
- honesty in exchanges with beloved
- provide advice and encouragement to men
- outlive men
- responsible
- live within the constraints of restrictions imposed by others
- woman and minister = connection between physical love and spiritual love
- respond to symbolic action imposed from outside
- moral model (Mary, Hester)
- supernatural aspect (Mistress Hibbins and ghost)
- limited power of action
- compassion (woman in crowd, Elizabeth)

These points are listed informally, with no attempt at parallel structure because, at this time, the nature of their relationships is still unestablished.

On a colored card (or a larger slip of paper), students write their centering sentence(s). Considering the points they have listed in relation to the center(s) they have defined for their papers, they experiment with design, moving the cards around a large flat surface. They are not seeking *order*, they are seeking the *shape* formed by relationships. Inclusion and arrangement of this material depends upon the central issue of inquiry and upon the points included.

For example, are all the ideas fairly equal in importance? If so, a writer whose center is the difference between appearance and reality in the male and female roles as presented by the two texts might choose to follow a point-by-point arrangement:

- Hester appears honest and straightforward, but she does not tell Dimmesdale about the return of Chillingworth.
- Women appear to be involved with supernatural powers; what other explanations does Hawthorne suggest?
- Men appear to be spiritual leaders. Are they for Elizabeth and for Hester?
- Elizabeth and Hester appear to have been separated from the men they love; their continued spiritual connection remains hidden until the end of the narratives. Their loyalty to their beloveds becomes evident at the moment of death.
- Hester and Elizabeth each appear to be exiled because of male decisions; yet each exercises her own free will, acting through a return (Hester to Boston, Elizabeth to Father Hooper's deathbed).

For this writer, the points balance one another. Each comment finds support in the texts; none is dependent upon another.

Once the points have arranged themselves into a pattern, the writer's task is to ask, "So what?" That is, what does this repetition of appearance and reality patterns reveal about Hawthorne's work in general or about these two texts in particular?

Another writer working from the same list of points might choose to examine the physical and spiritual isolation of women in the same texts by taking each character in turn. Here, one obvious pattern is to move from the less to the more important. The paper might begin with some of the secondary characters in *The Scarlet Letter:* Mistress Hibbins, who is isolated by bizarre behavior and rumors of her connections to the devil, and the compassionate young goodwife in the crowd who alone speaks in Hester's behalf (and who is dead by the final scaffold scene). The paper might then treat Elizabeth, who is marginalized by her minor role in the story and yet important because of the moral values she carries. She is isolated by her love for Parson Hooper and her unwillingness to accept marriage to him while he wears his veil, but, contrary to readers' expectations, she remains true throughout his life. Concluding with Hester, the most fully developed character, the paper might suggest that Hester experiences many of the aspects of isolation that have been imposed on the other women.

The same list of points lends itself to the development of other papers, as well. A paper examining the various roles of men and women might shape itself by contrasting each role. A paper dealing with the connections between spiritual and physical love might take each narrative in turn, comparing the relationships between the women and the ministers. By using diagramming cards to make the facts organize themselves, students discover that facts generalize themselves as well. As the arrangement of information emerges, so do critical insights, implications, and generalizations imbedded in the facts.

Students are now ready to draft independently. This particular sequence comes early in the semester, and, because student papers typically include direct quotations (attributable, no doubt, to the text search), we spend class time learning to handle them. We examine conventions of punctuation, indentation, and parenthetical citation by looking at passages from drafts-in-process. Students learn and practice a three-part pattern for smoothly integrating and effectively using quotations: (1) introduce the quotation; (2) present the quotation; and (3) comment on the significance of the passage quoted. The final step—making a comment—is the one that beginning writers neglect most often. They may work apt passages smoothly into their texts, but they leave the reader to fill in the connections to their points. Helping students with quotations while they are in the process of drafting avoids many difficulties in the final paper. Students learn while doing and, because the teaching is timely, need little later review.

Before publication, students respond to one another's drafts in groups. These groups are different from those in which they have been working so far; by this point, the prewriting group is intimately familiar with the topic and too familiar with each members' planning to be able to provide the alien views that give writers the most helpful feedback.

How effective is this sequence of activities? Here is the initial freewriting of one student. (Italics indicate the key ideas she checked when she reviewed her writing.)

Hawthorne Paper

> I have decided to compare Hawthorne's use of a central symbol in one of his short stories and *The Scarlet Letter*. I am planning to explore the symbol of the Scarlet Letter of Hester Prynne and the Black Veil of the minister and how it helps them see through different eyes. These symbols are obviously central because *they appear in the titles of the works*. In *The Scarlet Letter,* the public forces the Scarlet Letter to be put on Hester's breast. With the visible markings of a sinner, everyone knows that Hester is not "pure." People shun her and isolate her from society so that *her status becomes lowered*. It is at this point that she sees through different eyes. Before her sin was known, she was within society and didn't think much of the less unfortunate and poor and sick people that lived in the town. but when she was cast out and shunned, *she became one of the less fortunate*. She saw the town through different eyes. She saw them as cruel people who either ignored her or cast her away from them. *She noticed the poor and the sick and she helped them*. Society might ignore them, but Hester Prynne was not going to leave those who needed her without any help.
>
> In the "Minister's Black Veil," the Minister, for some unknown reason, but probably because he has sinned, dons a black veil. Before he had the veil, the story tells that his speeches were not out of the ordinary. It seemed *he could not relate to those in his parish*. He couldn't see their problems as they saw them. After he puts on the veil, he not only physically sees things in a different perspective, but we see *he literally sees through different eyes as his speeches become more and more popular with the people in his parish*. He also can understand the emotions of others.

This young lady was fluent, and her writing was rich in ideas. Not surprisingly, her contributions to discussion had been insightful from the beginning of the course. However, until this assignment, her formal papers had been safe and ordinary in content and linear in form. Typically, she would have taken this information, created a thesis statement such as "The scarlet letter and the black veil are two central symbols that help Hester Prynne and the minister see through different eyes." She might have devoted the next paragraph to a (potentially meagerly supported) discussion of how Hester learns to see through different eyes. The paragraph after that might have discussed the minister and his improved ability to inspire his parishioners. In her final paragraph, she might have restated her original thesis. Her paper—four paragraphs long—would have been predictable to any but the least discerning reader.

Here is what she did instead:

To See Through Different Eyes

In *The Scarlet Letter* and "The Minister's Black Veil," Hawthorne uses the scarlet letter and the black veil to enable the wearer to see through a different perspective. These symbols are central because not only are they included in the titles of the works, but they are constantly the focus of the works. Every detail relates in one way or another to the scarlet letter on Hester Prynne's breast in *The Scarlet Letter* and to the black veil hiding Father Hooper's face in "The Minister's Black Veil." Hawthorne's central symbols change in both function and effect as time passes.

In the beginning, both Hester Prynne and Father Hooper don the scarlet letter and the black veil, respectively, as a confession or supposed confession of a sin. The initial function of these symbols is to teach the wearer from their own sins by having a constant reminder. The effects on the wearer are immediate. In *The Scarlet Letter,* Hester is "without a friend on earth who [would dare] show himself."

Society demeans Hester to the point that there is not a single person that declares Hester Prynne a friend. She is cast out of society, and the townspeople shun her. Even as Hester tries to associate with society, "there [is] nothing that made her feel as if she [belongs] to it... as if she [inhabits] another sphere." The townspeople do not welcome her. On the contrary, they shun her and isolate her for her scarlet letter until she feels alone. Even when Hester tries to redeem herself with her helpful needlework, no one calls her to "embroider the white veil which [is] to cover the pure blushes of a bride," showing that the townspeople will never think of her as a "pure" person, only a defiled one. No matter how hard she tries, she will never be a part of society.

In "The Minister's Black Veil," Father Hooper experiences immediate isolation from the villagers. No one in his parish "[would aspire] to the honor of walking by their pastor's side." The villagers don't want to associate with the minister because of his black veil. Even "Old Squire Saunders... [would neglect] to invite Mr. Hooper to his table, where the good clergyman [has] been wont to bless the food, almost every Sunday since the settlement." The villagers are isolating him from his daily routine only because of his veil. "Children

[flee] from his approach" and adults stare at him, but never speak. Father Hooper is living in a desolate world with no friends and no family. Even his fiancée leaves him because of the black veil. He is alone and cannot fit into society any more.

As time passes, the function of these symbols changes. They let the wearers see through different eyes, letting them relate to other people. In *The Scarlet Letter* Hester Prynne feels that "the scarlet letter [endows] her with a new sense.... [It gives] her a sympathetic knowledge of the hidden sin in other hearts." Because of her scarlet letter on her breast, Hester is able to "see" those who sin. She has the kind of sympathetic feeling for them that only one who experiences the punishment of sin can feel. She is able to relate and feel for those with a sin only because of the scarlet letter she wears. The scarlet letter also helps her relate to the poor and sick in town. Because of the scarlet letter, Hester is another outcast, like the destitute, whom the townspeople regard with very little concern. Hester "sees" the poor and understands their position in society and their feelings as they are not much different from herself. Seeing that they cannot help themselves, Hester tries her best to help them. No one was as eager as Hester "to give of her little substance to every demand of poverty" and no one "so [helpful] as Hester, when pestilence [stalks] through the town." She is always willing to help the poor. She sews clothes for them and tends to their needs as much within her ability as she can. The effect of the scarlet letter on Hester is to make her a sympathetic, caring, and understanding person. She even receives the title of a "Sister of Mercy." The scarlet "A," in the hearts of those that she helps will always mean the "Able" Hester Prynne.

In "The Minister's Black Veil," the veil also enables Father Hooper to not only physically see through a different perspective, but he can also see through different eyes. The first sermon he says with the black veil draping his face is the minister's "most powerful effort." The black veil immediately had effect on the wearer, making him an energetic and a strong preacher. Besides "making its wearer a very efficient clergyman," the black veil also enables him "to sympathize with all dark affections."

The minister has most likely committed a sin. Feeling the weight of his sin upon him, he could feel for and understand the dark affections that afflict others because his situation is not much different from their own. With the black veil as a constant reminder, he suffers daily for his sin and can relate to those who have a guilty conscience about their sin. The black veil also transforms Father Hooper into "a man of awful power over souls that [are] in agony for sin." Father Hooper

> is the only one in the village who admits his sin. As a result, he is the only one who can outwardly console those who sin. The other villagers will not admit their sins so they would not have the same effect as the minister. Because the minister was sincerely understanding, he was the only one who could relieve the sin of another. It is the black veil that gives him such power. It helps him understand and relate to the villagers and helps him help society.
>
> In *The Scarlet Letter* and "The Minister's Black Veil," Hawthorne uses the central symbols of the scarlet letter and the black veil to enable the wearer to see through different eyes. Although at first Hester Prynne and Father Hooper suffer for their sins, they learn to see through a different perspective. Because of this, they serve the community and do the best for society.
>
> SHERI TSUDA

Several points are worth noting. First, in the original freewriting, Sheri made no explicit connection between the ways in which the scarlet letter and the veil force the respective communities to re-vision Hester and the minister; all she noted was that they caused Hester and the minister to see anew. The sequence of activities in and out of class enabled the generation of at least one new understanding for this student.

This paper considers several points rather than just one. It looks at the centrality of the symbols, how each forces its wearer to gain new perspective, and how the symbols change in function and effect. The development is hardly linear. Sheri discusses the symbols' initial function as a confession of sin, looks at the effects of the scarlet letter on Hester, examines the effect of the veil on the minister, considers the changing functions and effects of the symbols, first on Hester and then on the minister, and, finally, in her conclusion, pushes to a new idea: the scarlet letter and the black veil enable their wearers to "serve the community and do the best for society." The development, while complex, is clear and easy for a reader to follow.

Other students also found the assignment sequence effective. Evaluating it, one wrote:

> The discussion showed me where my weaknesses may have been when I couldn't always back my ideas with references to the text.

Students need practice handling assertions and evidence. They need to be challenged on their logic and questioned on the connections they make. The group talk before drafting provides that practice.

The sequence helped another student figure out a coherent reading of the text. He said, "I understood what I was trying to mean with my ideas, that before... made hardly any sense." Often, students notice details in their reading but have difficulty establishing relationships or a sense of relative importance. Using the diagramming cards and getting feedback from a group helped this student take his bits and pieces of information and create the patterns that formed the basis of his critical discourse.

Collaborative engagement and collaborative feedback are central to the success of the sequence. As another student wrote, "We were able to compare our ideas, and we began to pass [from] the factual into the theoretical." Moving from the factual to the theoretical, students move from reading to interpretation. They move from being textual receivers to critical inquirers. That is the experience, that is the movement, I seek to repeat.

9 Sequencing Inquiry into Poetry

The following sequence is designed for students untrained in (and uncomfortable with) reading poetry. Students begin with what they know, and a collaborative community of literary inquirers provides support and feedback as they practice poetic analysis and critical discourse. This extensive experience with collaborative inquiry also serves a larger function, helping students experientially recognize the indeterminacy of texts and the communal nature of critical inquiry.

Two activity strands allowing students several weeks with Emily Dickinson and her work constitute the sequence. In the *group strand,* students first explore Dickinson's biography and then graduate to reading and discussing her poems. As part of this strand, students are exposed to some critical viewpoints regarding Dickinson's work and introduced to basic strategies of poetic analysis. In the parallel *individual strand,* students work through an independent exploration of a single poem. At the end of the sequence, the strands merge in the writing, publication, and discussion of an analysis essay.

The two strands can be visualized as forming a double helix.

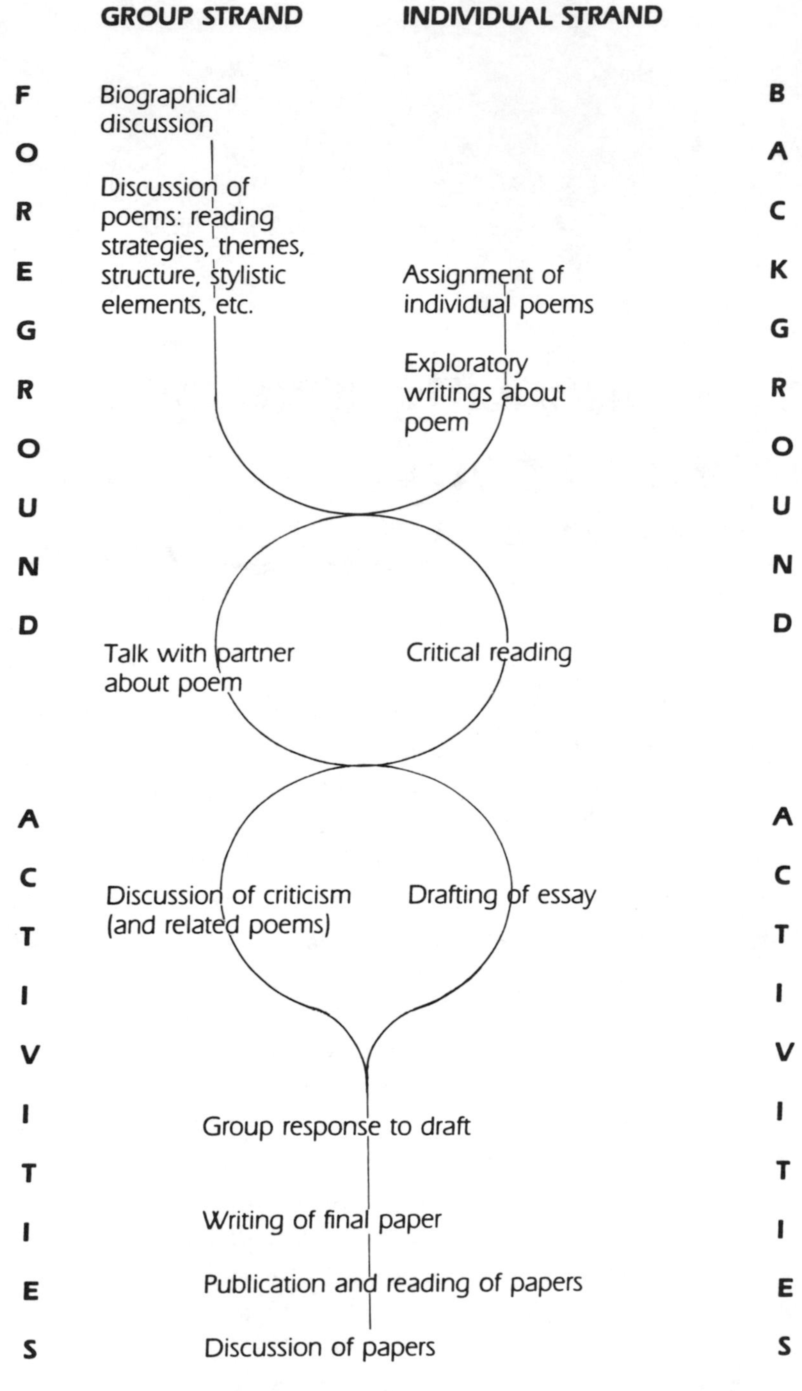

Figure 9–1 A Poetry Sequence

Each strand moves from the foreground to the background of class attention at different times. The strands parallel, reinforce, and interact with one another before merging in the culminating activities of the sequence. Issues that students discuss as a group inform their work with individually assigned poems. They, in turn, come to class with transferable observations from their personal work. Final papers are rich because students mine poems repeatedly but also because, by the end of the two strands, they have a sense of Dickinson's concerns and her methods of exploration. They have legitimate ways to place their observations of a single poem into the context of Dickinson's oeuvre.

Figure 9–1 provides an overview of a sequence design suitable for a course where students meet daily for fifty-minute periods and are expected to do thirty to forty-five minutes of homework every night. Please note that this is just one possible design among many. Activities can be rearranged, a sequence might include more or fewer poems, or students might do more or less critical reading.

In this sequence, we begin with the group strand establishing context. Several days before any discussion of Dickinson or her work, students do the first group activity.

GROUP ACTIVITY 1

- Read the introductory biographical material about Emily Dickinson in your text. Take notes on anything you feel interesting or important. Then go to the library and read as much as you can about Emily Dickinson and her life. You may find the first part of Cynthia Griffin Wolff's book, *Emily Dickinson* (New York: Alfred A. Knopf, 1986) interesting. Note information that intrigues you and that you think may inform your classmates. That is, try to find material that may be new to the rest of us. We will be sharing this information in class on [insert date]. You will be handing in your findings for credit/no credit that same day. Use appropriate MLA bibliographic form to cite each of your sources.

We accomplish a great deal with this activity. First, its mildly competitive tone ("find material that may be new") challenges students to go beyond basic information. During class discussion of the students' findings, a sense of Dickinson as a person (rather than a list of biographical statistics) tends to emerge. Second, giving students one current source does two things: (1) those who are timid in the library have a starting place; and (2) my bibliographical entry includes all the necessary information and so provides a model for students. Asking students to practice using proper bibliographical form reminds them that keeping track of sources of information is an important part of scholarship. Finally, the activity has a useful—and collaborative—end. This is not an empty exercise; its purpose is to inform the group. Students are held accountable for doing the work, but they also are given space in which to practice and opportunity to learn from one another.

On the first day of discussion, we go around the class circle and share findings. My job is to receive information, connect it to other things that we know or will learn, contribute when appropriate, and modify student offerings when the occasion suggests. For example, I might say, "Many biographers have agreed with Chris that Dickinson's mother was weak and lacked influence with her daughter, but others—Cynthia Wolff, for example—have questioned that view. Did anybody else in the class address that issue?" (if not, I may do so).

Examine what the discussion accomplishes. Students read the biography in their text and more, with themselves and a larger audience in mind. They read looking for information interesting to themselves and to their classmates, often probing deeply to find it, and learn a great deal about Emily Dickinson in the process. They take responsibility for how much biographical material they read as well as responsibility for discussion. They establish themselves as participating members of a critical community. The principles introduced in this activity underlie the entire sequence: all work is student centered and collaborative; it is focused yet allows room for individual shaping; and it is functional.

The second activity in the sequence introduces students to a poem and starts them thinking about strategies of reading poetry.

GROUP ACTIVITY 2

- Read J-324, "Some keep the Sabbath..." several times. Write a process log for the poem. First, identify the subject of the poem and briefly state what you think the poet is saying about it. Then describe as fully as possible the *process* of your reading.

The order in which I assign Dickinson's poems is idiosyncratic; some have favor partly because I like how I can make them work in my classes. I like to begin with this one because it is long enough to give students ample opportunities to make observations about their reading processes, yet short enough to be accessible on the first day of discussion.

Discussion begins with students reading their process logs. (Because such sharing is habitual in my classes, student reluctance about reading aloud disappears early in the course.) Before they start, I suggest that they note any reading strategies that seem potentially useful. After students finish sharing their reading processes, I offer the following progression for poetic analysis:

1. Examine the subject. What is this poem about?
2. Identify the stance. What are the poet's attitudes toward the subject(s)?
3. Put this particular poem in a thematic context. Does this subject represent a repeated concern?
4. Examine the structure. What is the verse form? Are there parallel elements, and, if so, how are they working? What are the progressions of time and space? Of attitude? How does the end of the poem extend or revise meaning?
5. Examine stylistic elements. Is the presentation simple or complex? What kind of images are used? Allusions? Irony and paradox? How are meter and rhyme working? In Dickinson's case especially, how are punctuation and capitalization being used?

In our discussion of Dickinson's work in upcoming classes, we follow this progression, beginning with general statements of subject, stance, and thematic content (what is being said), then moving to comments on structure and style (how it is being said). Repeating this pattern and making it explicit not only helps students internalize a way of organizing their probes into a poem but provides a model for the part-to-whole analysis that will be required in their papers later.

During the next few days, students read J-1052 ("I never saw a Moor—") and J-303 ("The Soul selects her own Society—"). The first poem is quite short, so I have students copy it and respond to it in a dialogue journal (GROUP ACTIVITY 3). In class, they break into groups to share their comments, noticings, and questions; each group then chooses the comments it finds most provocative to offer for class consideration. The next poem, J-303, is longer, and students write a reading response to it (GROUP ACTIVITY 4). Once again, student writing forms the basis for class discussion the next day.

At this point in the sequence, students have experienced three ways of writing in response to poems, they have used their writing as the basis of critical conversation, and they have had several opportunities to practice part-to-whole analysis. They are ready to begin the individual strand of the sequence.

Each student is asked to choose a different poem. I have found the following poems particularly useful for examination:

- J-49 "I never lost as much but twice"
- J-76 "Exultation is the going"
- J-160 "Just lost, when I was saved"
- J-214 "I taste a liquor never brewed"
- J-288 "I'm Nobody! who are you?"
- J-318 "I'll tell you how the Sun rose"
- J-333 "The Grass so little has to do"
- J-341 "After great pain, a formal feeling comes"
- J-449 "I died for Beauty"
- J-478 "I had no time to hate"
- J-585 "I like to see it lap the Miles"
- J-986 "A narrow Fellow in the Grass"
- J-1100 "The last Night that She lived"
- J-1624 "Apparently with no surprise"

Once students have made their choices, I give them the following directions:

INDIVIDUAL ACTIVITY 1

EXPLORING ON YOUR OWN

This project gives you an opportunity to become intimately acquainted with a poem by one of our finest lyric poets. In addition, you will become the class expert on your personal poem.

There will be a sequence of activities dealing with your poem. It is important that you do each activity as it is assigned and that you spend the suggested time on each sequence part. Here are your first directions:

Spend twenty minutes with your poem. During the first ten minutes, read the poem over several times. Mark it, making notes about anything you notice. Draw a line down the center of a page (or fold the paper lengthwise) and, using only the left side, write a process log of your reading. Remember to begin with a statement of the poem's subject and then describe, as best you can, how you came to understand the poem.

The first activities in both strands are designed to lead students to repeated engagement with texts. They are reminded that poems demand several readings and experience first-hand the benefits of multiple reentries. In the individual strand, students begin by responding in a form with which they are already familiar (the process log). However, asking students to write on only half the page (as they do in a dialogue journal) alerts them to a new use of the process log.

For the next several days, class discussion of different poems continues, following established patterns; students are asked to do expressive writing—dialogue journals, process logs, and reading responses—to prepare for these discussions. On their own, they work through two other individual activities.

INDIVIDUAL ACTIVITY 2

- Spend another twenty minutes with your poem. Read it over several times, then, again using only the left-hand side of the page, as in the last assignment, write a reading response in which you summarize the poem's action(s), respond to the feelings it evokes, and explore its imagery.

Once again, students are asked to respond in a familiar way but with a variation.

The reading response is particularly useful for broad explorations of feelings and imagery. I next have students enter a dialogue with their first two pieces of expressive writing.

INDIVIDUAL ACTIVITY 3

- Return to what you wrote in response to Activities 1 and 2. Using the right-hand side of the page, have a conversation with yourself about your writing. Ask yourself questions, negate your assertions, comment on your comments. Push your ideas in as many different directions as you can.

Here, students have a chance to experience a variation on the dialogue journal. Having done a process log and a reading response, they engage in conversation with the observations that they made earlier. They have a chance to revise their thinking, question earlier assumptions, and examine their critical processes.

The next activity allows students a more imaginative experience with their poems.

INDIVIDUAL ACTIVITY 4

- Write an imitation of your poem. Keep the original shape and patterns of punctuation as best you can, but use your own subject and your own language. Can you use capitalization the same way Dickinson does? When you have an effort that satisfies, spend ten minutes freewriting about the two poems and what you learned from the imitation.

Doing imitations of the poems provides interiority and is particularly useful when students are working with poetry, because poetry as a form makes them uneasy. When they experience the poem from the inside out, they are able to feel themselves creatively aligned with Dickinson.[1]

At this point, students are ready to distance themselves and approach the poem from a keenly analytical vantage point.

INDIVIDUAL ACTIVITY 5

- Spend twenty minutes with your poem. During the first ten minutes, read it aloud several times. Listen to the rhythms and sounds it makes. Begin to memorize it. Spend the next ten minutes writing about how the sound is used to reinforce feelings and images. What use does Dickinson make of

> punctuation and capitalization to help the reader understand sound patterns?

When students memorize a passage, they internalize observations of which they often are not consciously aware. They begin to recognize how particular rhythms and sounds evoke emotional responses. They understand how capitalization and punctuation create the ragged rhythms that Dickinson commonly used for thematic underscoring.

Here is how one student responded after her exploration of J-76 "Exultation is the going...":

> In the first quatrain, Dickinson introduces us to the idea that "Exultation is the going of an inland soul to sea." Exultation is a very strong word describing how excited we are to go to sea. She emphasizes this feeling by softening the rest of the line with the alliteration of "soul to sea." Also, by ending in an "e" sound, she leads us to the next two lines, "past the houses—past the headlands—into deep Eternity." In these lines, Dickinson uses the dashes to symbolically lead to eternity. The dashes also serve the purpose of emphasizing the length of eternity. She goes from a short "past the houses" and "past the headlands" into a rather long "into deep Eternity."

Despite the limited time and a minimum of direction, this student discovered aspects of the poem that might well have remained hidden to her if her only exposure to the poem had been one or two readings in search of "hidden meanings." Not only did she understand *what* the poem is saying, but she was learning to notice *how* it works. Her insights are remarkably sophisticated for a sixteen-year-old.

She was not alone in her powers of poetic discernment. Another student responded to J-214 this way:

> "I taste a liquor never brewed," "Inebriate of Air—am I—," and "Not all the Vats upon the Rhine yield such an alcohol" are all key lines in the poem because they support the idea of a natural inebriation. The fact that "Air" is capitalized shows us that Dickinson was trying to stress this word. Throughout the poem, the author makes sure that these capitalized words state the same idea. Each one contributes to

> the message that Dickinson herself lives by the philosophy of non-alcoholic happiness.

Not only was this student aware that capitalization creates emphasis, he noticed Dickinson's consistent capitalization of the same words and concluded, properly, that the emphasis is intended to lead us to meaning.

The next activity keeps students looking closely at their poems but shifts the direction of their attention.

INDIVIDUAL ACTIVITY 6

- Again spend twenty minutes with your poem. Continue to work on memorization. Spend your last ten minutes writing about the use of structure and diction in the poem.

Students must be taught to consider the weight of individual words in a piece. In a similar fashion, they need help looking at how structure—stanza development, line breaks, and rhyme scheme—works to generate and underscore poetic meanings. One student's insights into J-478, "I had no time to Hate" were particularly adroit:

> The first stanza's construction and diction form part of its message. The mid-sentence breaks between lines and the awkwardness of their position seems to disrupt the train of thought and draws the reader's attention to the message of each line by disturbing the rhythm of the poem. The awkward breaks in addition to the slant rhyme between "hinder Me" and "Enmity" seem to be indicative of the imperfectness of hate for the shortness of life.

A second student concentrated his attention on rhyme scheme and how it functions in "To Hear an Oriole Sing" (J-525):

> One technique used in the poem was rhyme scheme. The poem consisted of five verses of three lines each. In each of the first four verses, the first two lines of each verse rhymed. However, the last line of each verse broke the pattern and that somehow made the thought seem unfinished or imperfect because the verse is imperfect as far as the rhyme scheme goes. The last verse is perfect, rhyme-wise, and this

> seems fitting because the last verse wraps up all the ideas into the main idea that was trying to be made all along, just like perhaps the rhyme was trying to be made all along.

A scant ten minutes focused on structure and diction allowed both of these students to make some important observations. They are learning questions to ask of poems, areas of focus for critical inquiry. Their probes are richly rewarded.

At this juncture, students have finished independent explorations of their poems. They have examined the process of their reading and their personal feelings; they have summarized their poem's action, thought about its imagery, and considered structural and stylistic issues. They are ready for feedback. The individual strand of the sequence now moves from the background of class attention to the foreground. Students spend a period working in pairs, each reading the other's poems, and then listening to their partners' explications. The experts explain as much as possible about their assigned poem. The novices ask as many questions as they can. Depending on time and group needs, this process could be repeated once or twice, with students talking to two or three different classmates during a period.

After students have had a chance to test their understandings of their poems on their classmates, the individual strand once again moves into the background, with the next activity.

INDIVIDUAL ACTIVITY 7

- Finish memorizing your poem, and prepare to recite it. Write a clean draft of a paper in which your purpose is to share a coherent reading of your poem with your classmates and to analyze the poem, showing how it fits into the context of Dickinson's work and how structure and stylistic elements combine to shape its meaning.

Students need several days to work on paper drafts. During that time, we expand our critical community by bringing in essays from professional journals. Students receive the following directions:

GROUP ACTIVITY 5

- Find an article on Emily Dickinson that interests you and treats the poet and/or her work in general terms. Although passing reference to a poem we have worked with individually or as a group is all right, don't choose an article that centers its discussion on one of our poems. Write a brief summary (no more than a page) of your article. You will be sharing this in class. Cite the source of your article, using proper bibliographic form.

This activity gives the class an excellent opportunity to explore the views of professional critics without being overwhelmed by them. Students have already done much exploration on their own, individually and in the group, and typically find that the critics reaffirm much of what they have already determined themselves. This adds to their confidence as readers.

Furthermore, the activity expands student inquiry and shows them that critical writing is a way of participating in literary discussion. I ask students to present their summaries one by one. After the first has done so, we see if anyone else had a commentary that deals with the same issues. If so, we discuss that one next, working to establish where the two positions agree and disagree. Typically, as the conversation develops, the order of sharing becomes organic, with students offering to read when they recognize that their summaries fit with the one just read. In addition, since Dickinson's poems are short, when articles discuss poems that we have not read, we take the opportunity to read them then.

Without sending students to do the kind of critical reading that can get in their way when they are shaping their own views, this activity acquaints them with the discussions that revolve around a particular writer. This widening of the critical community they seek to join correspondingly broadens their thinking as they continue work on their drafts.

The remainder of the sequence merges the individual strand and the group strand as papers near completion. Students bring the drafts to class and, after reciting their poems to a partner, share their papers with a response group. I give them the following directions:

1. Slowly and clearly read your paper to your group. Discuss your poem with them, answering any questions your paper didn't. Does the group agree with your analysis? Keep a written record of the questions and comments they have.

2. Keeping in mind your group's response, revise your paper to type and hand in. Do you need to revise the order of your points? Do you need to clarify ideas or sentence structure? Is your reading valid? Clear? Interesting? Have you handled quoted material properly?

3. Please type your name directly under the title of your paper; papers will be duplicated to form a class publication.

The completed essays are bound to form a class anthology, a copy of which is given to each member. Students then read everyone's work, using the anthology as a starting point for a class summary of Dickinson and her work. Here are two complete essays.

Emily's Riddle

Emily's Dickinson's poem J-986, "A narrow Fellow in the Grass," is a carefully written poem which uses many techniques to achieve its overall effect. The effect of the poem is to create images of a snake in the reader's mind.

A very interesting aspect of this poem is that it is written much like a riddle would be written. Dickinson seems to be asking the reader to identify the "narrow Fellow" that she describes. A snake fits the description nicely. Dickinson uses imagery to lead the reader to the conclusion that she is talking about a snake. The first line, "A narrow Fellow in the Grass," immediately conjures up images of the old snake in the grass. The second stanza's second line also is descriptive of a snake: "A spotted shaft is seen—." Further, there are images such as that of the grass dividing "as with a Comb—" which lead to a picture of something thin sliding through the grass. Also in the third stanza there is the line "It wrinkled, and was gone—" which also adds to that snake image. Thus, purely through imagery, Dickinson is able to generate the idea of a snake in the reader's mind without ever mentioning the word "snake" or "serpent."

Dickinson also uses stylistic elements to give the poem a snake-ish feeling. For instance, Dickinson uses enjambment and that makes the lines run together in one continuous flow. Also, there are no periods in the poem so there is no stop anywhere. The whole poem is one long line, just like a snake.

Other stylistic elements that Dickinson uses are alliteration and assonance to make the lines flow together. Particularly there are many repeated "s" sounds. An example of this is line two of the second quatrain: "A spotted shaft is seen—." Notice the s's in the last four words. As one reads the line aloud there is a definite hissing sound made. The "o" and "oo" sounds are also abundant as in the third through fifth lines of the third stanza: "A Floor too cool for Corn—/ Yet when a Boy and Barefoot—/I more than once at Noon." The effect of the repetition of sound is that the poem slides, hisses and slithers around as it is read aloud.

The meaning of the poem lies mostly in the last two quatrains. In effect, what Dickinson is saying is that although she is familiar with a number of animals, and she has a general feeling of friendship with most animals, the snake has always been a source of excitement for her. That excitement seems to stem from fear. The two important lines are the last two: "Without a tighter breathing/ And Zero at the Bone—." Dickinson gets excited and breathes funny. The "Zero at the Bone" is a way of saying that she feels like she has no bones, or she's scared, just like the saying, "You have no backbone."

The overall effect of the poem is that Dickinson is asking the reader a riddle. The riddle describes a snake through the use of imagery and sound. Dickinson also conveys to the reader a wonderment and fear of the snake that she experiences whenever she meets one.

MICHAEL KATO

This essay has a strong, personal voice. It is the work of a student who had connected with the poem, tapped many of its levels, and felt confident about his reading. Michael noticed some interesting aspects of the poem, particularly the way it works as a riddle and the ways the sound mimics snake movement and snake sound. I returned to this poem with heightened sensitivity as a result of his enlightening observations and was delighted that one of my students had forced me to do so!

Other student essays often have similar effects. Indeed, one of the side benefits of a collaborative classroom is that a teacher's readings are enriched by students. Students notice things in texts that we don't. They can illuminate aspects of a story or poem that previously lay in shadow. Potentially, they teach us while we teach them.

The following essay is one that taught me. When I finished reading it, I settled back in my chair, feeling pleased that my teaching had not gotten in the way of the production of such fine critical work.

"I Taste a Liquor Never Brewed..."

In an introduction to Emily Dickinson, the writer states that, "In her poems Emily Dickinson constructed her own world—of the garden." In Dickinson's poem, J-124, "I taste a liquor never brewed..." Dickinson creates a closely knit and attractive world filled with the wonders of Nature. Surrounded by the intricate and vast beauties of Nature, Emily Dickinson becomes drunk with them and because of them—drunk with "a liquor never brewed..." she believes that if you can find the beauty, significance, and wonders both great and small in Nature, then you won't have to get drunk to find happiness and peace; instead you will get drunk because of happiness.

These cheerful, comely connotations of nature appear in phrases such as: "Tankards scooped in Pearl," and "endless summer days," and "inns of Molten Blue" and "drunken bee" and "snowy hats." Most of these descriptions are metaphorical, and in fact, the whole poem is based on the metaphor that Nature is that untasted liquor both the poet and the bee are drunk on. One example of metaphorical usage occurs in the third stanza where a bee, intoxicated by the foxglove's nectar, is chased out of the foxglove, which is portrayed as a bar, because he is already too drunk.

One of Emily Dickinson's most common stylistic devices is the dash. In this poem, the meter alternates from iambic tetrameter to iambic trimeter, and the oddly placed dashes create an irregular, jerky rhythm, as if a drunk person was speaking, but found himself interrupted by unexpected hiccups.

Also, when a person is drunk, words tend to slur and get jumbled together. Emily Dickinson uses round-sounding words that are slurry and blurry, not crisp and cleanly cut. The round-sounding words are words such as: "summer," "molten," "Drunken," "Seraphs," and "Tippler." The round-sounding words are soft to the ear and mouth, and if you extend the pronunciation of the underlined sections, it sounds like a low murmur or hum, or even a drunken buzzing bee.

These round-sounding words draw the drunk poet, the drunk bee, and Nature all together, not only because the sounds slur together, but also because both Nature and the human world have the same characteristics. For example, the foxglove, which belongs to Nature, has a door, which is a human object; and saints and seraphs, who belong in heaven and are supposed to be perfect, are actually running and dashing like curious humans to see an odd sight, or swinging their hats like excited men.

Another message in this poem is one of subtle rebellion. First of all, in the 1860's the thought of an inebriated, debauched woman was quite unthinkable, and even today, that kind of woman would receive some attacks of scorn. Thus the poem is a rebellious call for women to taste an untasted liquor even better than the kind rowdy men order in a stuffy bar. Women can get their drinks anytime they want out in the open, without the crude, rash effects of alcohol. Women, who are more in touch and responsive to emotions, can taste this fine liquor simply through appreciation of Nature.

Another sign of rebellion appears in the third stanza where flowers chase the bees away when they should actually welcome the busy insect into their petal-bodies; and the butterflies, too, rebel against some unwritten law in nature by "renouncing their drams." The final stanza is also a rebellious one since the drunk woman and the drunk bee won't let themselves be handled by a stubborn man or flower: "I shall but drink the more!"

The effect of the "round-sounding" words and the rebellion of both a human and a bee creates a world that is related and altogether a very human place to be. Thus Nature is an intoxicating drink, and its effects run from a bee to heaven, and one can never get enough, nor will too much of the untasted, unbrewed liquor of Nature hurt anyone. The liquor is the liquor of life.

CHERYL IZUKA

I am impressed by the strong student voices in these essays. These students were no longer intimidated, either by the poem or by the critical commentary that surrounds it. The poems had become theirs. What they had to say is as valid as what anybody has to say. Delighted by their competence, I am enlightened by their insights.

Student response to the Dickinson sequence is always favorable. The activities build enjoyment and confidence. One student wrote, "I started out being very worried . . . because I don't always enjoy poetry." She then averred, "By the time I finished, I really enjoyed my poem." It seems safe to assume that her earlier lack of enjoyment might have been coupled with fear of failure or actual lack of success. Her eventual ownership of the poem (ownership she signals with the possessive adjective, "my") suggests both comfort and success.

A second student was equally explicit. He stated that "the best part about this process was that it helped build my confidence."

Confidence and enjoyment provided the nerve and the balance necessary for his evaluation of Dickinson and her work: "She was not a fancy poet, but a good one." I think Dickinson would have appreciated the judgment.

Built into the sequence are many opportunities for students to engage with their texts and to make records of those engagements. Writing the personal-response pieces forces students to keep track of their thoughts and the processes by which those thoughts emerge and develop. Some like the permanence their expressive writing provides. One noted, "By recording what I found, I couldn't lose my idea." He added that he "lost an idea" earlier and found it "frustrating." Ideas are precious commodities for students. They mistrust their ability to retain them or to generate new ones. A sequence of activities that includes multiple opportunities for writing helps with retention and shows students what fertile thinkers they really are. They are surprised by how many ideas they have.

The sequence also helps students generate material for their papers. "Reading the poem over and over many times is what really helped me to understand it," one wrote. Another agreed:

> The writing and the group work made us think of new ideas that our particular poem generated. . . . [We had to] think more because we had only one poem to work with.

The sequence forces students to return again and again to a work and teaches them not only about the poems themselves but about the value of repeated attention to critical analysis.

As with the Hawthorne sequence, students are faced with a plethora of material at once and are often unsure how to shape their papers. One wrote:

> When I was looking at my poem the previous week, I had only one understanding [of it]. But as I went on memorizing it and studying it, I came up with two more.

These extra ideas caused problems:

> I didn't know how to work my other ideas into my paper. So I left them out. . . . Now as I write this I wish that I had put them in.

This student was skilled in writing linear essays defending single assertions, but she lacked practice with having many interesting or useful things to say. She was still unwilling to risk working in a less tidy form.

Sequenced assignments complicate a teacher's job in many ways. Things become less tidy. We juggle many balls at a time: whole class, small group, and individual work; work with reading critically, with writing critically, and with talking collaboratively; work with concepts and with mechanics. Student responses to the literature become more complex (which is, after all, what we want), and we need to find ways to prepare students to deal with complexity, both on the sentence level and at the level of the whole text. They need practice to learn how to subordinate and relate ideas to produce balanced, coherent prose. They need to learn that the shape of discourse is infinitely plastic, changing to suit content.

When our teaching is successful, not only do our students engage with Dickinson, but they engage us as their readers. Repeated practice teaches them to be confident, sure of their readings and capable of skillful management of their material. Their critical commentaries become fresh and insightful. They are ready to be introduced to more complex critical strategies.

CONCLUSION

Sequenced activities help students spiral in and out of a text, connecting with it personally and distancing themselves from it critically. Sequences provide in-depth engagement with a writer and an oeuvre; students develop an extended context for critical discussion that is impossible from limited exposure. Useful sequence design recognizes students as beginners needing practice and reinforcement.

It is a commonplace that the shape of writing assignments determines the kinds of learning students experience. The sequences described in the preceding chapters are designed specifically for students inexperienced with critical inquiry. They help students perceive texts and their responses to them, and they enable students to share those perceptions communally. Their design emphasizes the movements fundamental to critical discourse.

Advanced students need to go beyond simple perception and validation, and we can design critical problems to help them do so. Critically experienced students might learn specific sequences of probes, patterns that they can employ to question texts. Composition theory, for example, provides heuristic probes for invention that transfer to critical exploration. For example, students can apply the questions raised by Aristotle's *topoi* ("topics," or "commonplaces") to critical inquiry and their examination of literary texts. Aristotle's *topoi* suggest four questions to ask. His first question asks students to classify a work by considering questions of genre. The question might lead them to differentiate and to look at how a particular work adapts or subverts generic convention. The same question might also lead students to other directions of inquiry. They might, for example, classify a work by author and look at how it differs from other texts by the same writer. A work could be classified by period and differentiated from other works of the period or from works of other periods.

Aristotle's second question, "What caused it?", might be answered in terms of a specific text (what were the motivating forces behind its creation?), or in terms of an event within a text (why did Hester Prynne refuse to reveal Dimmesdale as the father of her child?), or in terms of an effect a text has on the reader (how does the rhythm in Poe's poem "The Raven" contribute to the meanings of the piece?).

The third question, "What is it like?", asks for comparison (and, its negative, contrast). Here again attention might be directed historically, formally, or thematically. The question raises issues of context and intertextuality. It demands the inclusion of the individual work into larger patterns.

Aristotle's final question, "What do people say about it?", leads students to examine the discussion in a critical community. Reading what others have to say about texts or listening and responding to classmates' comments, students gather the testimony necessary to determine the validity of a particular reading of a text.

Kenneth Burke's Pentad (action, agent, means, purpose, and scene) provides another useful way of enriching critical inquiry. The Pentad's "action" requires thinking about plot as the subject of textual focus. Burke's notion of agent asks students to look at who is doing the action but also demands characterization of the narrative voice(s) of a text. "Means" asks students to wonder *how* the action is done, and suggests evaluation of the adequacy of means. "Purpose" gets students thinking about motivation: the characters', the author's, or theirs as readers. "Scene" properly includes consideration of both where and when and alerts readers to be sensitive to changes and sequences in location and time.

Without bogging students down with terminology, teachers can design activities during which students experience the thinking strategies these probes embody. They are simple to teach, simple to apply, and capable of helping students develop complex textual analysis.

Critical theory also offers explicit ways of thinking about literature. We can go beyond the comparison and analysis presented in the Hawthorne sequence or the explication developed in the Dickinson sequence (both grounded in a revised view of New Critical theory) to offer students experience with strategies used by more contemporary critics. Once again, we would probably do so without encumbering our younger or less experienced students with too much terminology or background.

We might borrow from Reader-Response theory and have students ask, "How does the language of the text work to create the experience of the reader?" We might use David Bleich's progression and ask students to identify the most important word, the most important passage, the most important feature in a text. This exercise would raise Bleich's fundamental question, "What does one mean by *the most important?*" (1975, 50) and help students deny "the priestly role critics have assigned themselves" (62–63). A Structuralist approach might involve asking students to analyze the patterns of Dickinson's poems and the embedded conventions of reading her work. Offering a Feminist approach would enable students to explore the two directions of literary feminism: (1) "an analysis of women attempting to write in a patriarchal culture"; and (2) exploration of a feminist aesthetic or "an explanation of how writing by women manifests a *distinctively* female discourse" (Davis 1986, 161).

The Hawthorne sequence and the Dickinson sequence could easily be expanded or redirected to offer students more sophisticated experiences with the texts than they currently do. Possibilities are multiple and exciting, both for students and for teachers.

BEYOND THE FUNDAMENTALS

10 Final Observations

Where do we go from here? James Moffett suggests that we ask ourselves, "How differently would you teach if your students did not *have* to come to class?" (1988, 5). Like merchants faced with selling a product, teachers in this position would have several alternatives. They could continue doing what they had been doing and hope that the clientele would remain obedient, friendly, and in attendance. They could turn to gimmicks—flashy equipment or jazzy presentations—to attract the audience. Or they could choose quality and simply provide the best possible educational experience for their students. It is hard to imagine serious educators choosing anything but the last course. Still, making that choice demands that we rethink the nature of our enterprise.

I want to return to Chapter 1, to the problems with student writing that reads like cold mashed potatoes. Roger's students were a typical high-school group, yet the deficiencies in their prose are shared by college undergraduates: lack of voice, focus, interest, and life. Sometimes, such writing even lacks appropriate content. I would suggest that the writing we get from students stems directly from our misconceptions regarding the nature of education and the resultant misdesign (or shortage) of learning experiences in language arts and English classes from kindergarten up.

We want our classrooms to be friendly, comfortable, and interesting places to work. We want the work to be productive and imaginative—worthwhile for students and for us. We want them to understand—and be driven by—the essential selfishness of education as a process engaged in for personal pleasure and benefit. We want students to recognize their obligation to educate one another, and us, as we engage in examination of the world. We want them to learn and to enjoy the process. When we accomplish this, we provide our students with high-quality educational experiences in which they would choose to participate, even if not compelled.

Considering Moffett's question with an eye to educational quality leads me to posit an answer. Students would want to come to literature class if they were convinced that membership in a club of critical inquiry had value for them. They would want to come if they could be assured of participating in real educational experiences—experiences that would lead to that membership—with classmates and the teacher.

This answer is risky because it demands that we change the existing power relationships between teacher and student. Neither teachers nor the academy they represent can continue to insist on absolute values, absolute truth, or absolute control. Our epistemology forces us to understand knowledge as something people construct collaboratively. Our psychological and pedagogical theory force us to recognize that learning is creative and connected directly to experience. Instead of thinking of lesson or unit plans in terms of discussion questions or skill drills, our new classroom forces us to think in terms of the educational experiences we offer students.

When we think of the educational experiences we provide, we need to think of teaching *students* as much as we think of teaching *content*. Two principles require careful consideration. First, learning needs to be both experienced and demonstrated. Students need to assimilate and to be made aware of their processes of assimilation. Second, in order to assimilate material, students need multiple opportunities to manipulate it. Typically, this manipulation takes place through the mediating powers of language use—reading, writing, talking, listening. Effective manipulation takes place through integrated language use in which all processes are complementary and connected.

Simply redesigning our classrooms to make them collaborative is not enough. We need to make them experiential as well. Students trained by teachers who feel that it is more important to cover material, to finish a text during a year, than to give students thought-provoking experiences with course content are trained to be superficial in their inquiries. Such students learn to read only to acquire facts, to garner material to regurgitate on a senseless series of short-answer or multiple-choice tests.

Reading to acquire information—what Louise Rosenblatt calls "efferent" reading (1978)—is, of course, a centrally useful educational skill. However, too much concentration on the information texts contain often blocks the experiences they provide. When students are not given time to experience a text, to develop a personal sense of it, and are pushed into analytical activities before they are ready, their analyses are predictably shallow. Their teachers wail, "These kids can't think!" They are right. But, given the setting, nobody could—they do not have a firmly established foundation on which to build. Students who ignore textual experience fail to learn how to read for aesthetic pleasure or critical engagement. They become adept at what Scardamalia calls "knowledge telling" but incapable of the active reworking of information, the critical reshaping that Scardamalia labels "knowledge transforming" (1984, 6). We claim that the critical transformation of material is a primary goal of our teaching, yet educational practice often works against the acquisition of habits of mind that enable such thinking.

Teachers who fail to recognize that the kinds of writing and talking activities they offer need to vary with the kind of learning they wish to promote typically train students into limited discoursers. Their students write obedient (and obvious), linear, thesis-driven argument papers but are confused and inept when faced with more complex rhetorical tasks. Forced to jam complex material into simple forms, they confront a problem of composition similar to one that William Carlos Williams described:

> Forcing twentieth-century America into a sonnet . . . is like putting a crab into a square box. You've got to cut his legs off to make him fit. When you get through, you don't have a crab any more. (1986, 365)

Content does not tuck itself tidily into prescribed forms. Providing students with only one form with which to respond to texts asks them to chop up the literature in the process.

In addition, standard writing assignments in many introductory literature courses lead students to seek single generalizations about complex texts. But students are apprentices, inexperienced with textual explorations. Their generalizations fail to satisfy because they are too general. When teachers (properly) view them as obvious and exhort students to "be specific," it is no wonder that students throw their hands up in despair and flee to other disciplines where the enterprise feels more coherent.

Students trained by teachers who are not themselves readers and writers are likely to be limited by their instructors' lack of experience. Such teachers may be unable to give students experiences with conversations among texts, and among readers, because the last ones in which they themselves participated occurred when they were students. Such teachers like their students, like teaching, and work hard. However, they invest their energies in activities that are less than optimally useful. Planning study questions and unit exams may be necessary but may not be as important as spending several hours with a novel, a new book of poetry, or even *The New Yorker*. Helping students master the usage conventions of written English is important, but perhaps some of the time spent correcting student papers might be employed as usefully working on an article for publication or a poem for personal pleasure. Teachers must not neglect personal literacy in their dedication to student competence. One informs the other.

Teachers who are not writers often blindly perpetuate artificial dicta regarding formal discourse. "Never use the personal pronoun *I*," they insist. Were they experienced writers, they might be more likely to acquaint students with ways in which overuse of *I* deflects attention from a subject to the voice that is discussing it. Instead of teaching students that passive voice is bad, they might help students see how it works to change the focus from the actor ("Sarah baked the cake") to the product of the action ("The cake was baked by Sarah").

Similarly, teachers who have struggled with the complexities of connecting sentences into coherently extended prose will be wary of arbitrarily forbidding one-sentence paragraphs and sentences that begin with present participles or coordinating conjunctions. Rather than legislating language use by fiat, teachers who write themselves can extend their students' facility with language by making them consciously aware of the implications of language variables. Appropriate language use, as writers know, cannot be described in absolute terms; it is always dependent upon context.

In the same way, a teacher who has written critical papers (or perhaps just read widely in the critical journals) will come to recognize that form is dependent upon content and that even the structure of the argument form varies in different contexts. Such a teacher might second Virginia Woolf's assertion that the essay is "the medium which makes it possible for people of ordinary intelligence to communicate their ideas to the world" (quoted in Anderson 1988, 150). Communication—the rich exchange of ideas—is what we are after. Formal validity must be measured against a pragmatic standard of what is interesting and effective communication.

Response to Moffett's question has led me to develop a classroom in which students make choices within the context of the educational objectives to be served. They have a sense of purpose about their classroom activities. Pedagogical focus is on what students can accomplish through reading, writing, and talking. All discourse modes are seen as vehicles for legitimate communication, not empty academic exercises. Procedures and routines are not taught in isolation but embedded in meaningful context.

I attempt to stretch students just beyond their current levels of maturation but do so by means of a series of guided activities that enable student success. Collaboration promotes these extensions.

Learning is social and communal. The role of teacher as sole evaluator is minimized so that it does not obstruct the role of student as learner. Control of the educational process shifts consciously and increasingly from the teacher to the student. The goal of the process is to move students from apprenticeship to independent expertise.

Such a model promotes learning that is meaningful, useful, collaborative, and risk free—all qualities characterizing the learning that people experience as participants in a group of similarly interested individuals.

The activities presented in this text—individually and in sequence—are designed for such an educational situation. They are structured to recognize that students are beginners, people in apprenticeship, and they provide scaffolding for that apprenticeship. They rest upon a belief that learning is a collaborative social activity. They strive to connect reading, writing, talking, and thinking in a fertile, generative critical process. They seek to make students independent, skillful, informed members of a club of critical inquirers. They are worth incorporating into every teacher's classroom practice, even though student attendance is mandatory.

Notes

Chapter 1. Reclaiming the Range of Critical Discourse

1. The tone of the directions given to students in texts as recent as twenty years old reveals that the notion of contingency had not yet found general acceptance. One text advises: "The thesis sentence is a good starting-point in the composition process because it forces the writer to determine at the outset just what it is that he wants to say about his chosen or designated subject. Moreover, it lays the foundation for a unified coherent discourse" (Corbett [1965] 1971, 48).

More recent texts are redefining their notions of thesis to accommodate contingency. In *The Random House Handbook*, Crews writes, "to the concept of the trial topic... we must add that of the *trial thesis*, a would-be leading idea which is still untested" (1984, 96). The schizophrenic confusion this paradigm shift is causing the textbook industry is apparent when a publisher attempts to modernize an old favorite by applying an overlay of new paradigm theory. For example, these two sentences appeared one after the other on the same page in a recently revised text:

> Although the thesis is often called a purpose statement, thesis and purpose are not precisely the same thing. Your purpose is both contained in and larger than your thesis; it is all the discoveries and decisions you have used to create that thesis, and all the strategies you will use to demonstrate it in a sustained and successful piece of writing.

and

> Your thesis is usually an overt, written-out statement. It makes a restricted, unified, and precise assertion about your subject—that is,

> an assertion that can be handled in the amount of space you have, that treats only one idea, and that is open to only one interpretation. (McCrimmon 1984, 27)

These two sentences are born of very different assumptions about writing, about thesis statements, and—one suspects—about contingency.

2. My informal survey of literature teachers (both high school and college) asked for a description of "the competent academic essay" (either student written or found in an academic journal), information about the function of such an essay, and a description of how it functions. Of the eight high-school teachers who responded, six suggested a valorization of the thesis-dominated essay, using terminology such as "argue convincingly," "appropriate thesis," "an assertion," "stated clearly in a thesis," and "a unifying thesis." College professors revealed a greater degree of discomfort with formal limitations. However, academic privileging of the argument form at the university level is evident when schools like Pennsylvania State University design required composition courses devoted entirely to developing argument skills (Fahnestock and Secor 1983).

Textbooks focused specifically on writing literary analysis similarly center attention on thesis and its control of content. Three such specialized texts are *Writing about Literature* (Cohen 1973), *Writing about Imaginative Literature* (Gordon 1973), and *Writing Themes about Literature* (Roberts 1983), whose discussions of critical writing are firmly grounded within the conventions of the thesis-dominated argument form. A newer publication, Sylvan Barnet's *A Short Guide to Writing about Literature* (1985), suggests a more generous and open role for the literary critic, as well as a wider range of composing possibilities. Consequently, it does not place notions of thesis in the foreground, although the issue is addressed.

3. Indeed, that is precisely the effect of textbook statements such as "the beginning of all discourse is a subject. . . . Obviously, no decisions about expression can be made until one's subject matter has been clearly defined" (Corbett [1965] 1971, 45). The text continues:

> Simple as the principle is, many students have difficulty in framing their thesis in a single declarative sentence. Part of their difficulty stems from the fact that they do not have a firm grasp on their ideas before they sit down to compose a thesis sentence. (49)

4. Anthony Petrotsky similarly redefines the notion of "main idea" when applied to interpretation. He says, "it is only useful to talk about 'main idea' where main idea represents a guess at the consensus understanding of a particular group (like test makers) reading for a particular purpose" (1986, 3).

5. Authorities on assignment design and assignment sequencing often argue for placing activities in a developing progression. Many build their sequences on Benjamin Bloom's (1956) taxonomy of thinking skills—knowledge, comprehension, application, analysis, synthesis, and evaluation. James Moffett takes a rhetorical approach based on a series of relationships among writer, subject, and audience (1983, 1988). Composition texts are typically arranged in a progression (from description and narration to definition and argument) similarly based on increasing difficulty.

Kahn, Walter, and Johannessen (1984) owe their sequences to "A Taxonomy of Skills in Reading and Interpreting Fiction" (Hillocks and Ludlow 1984). Their sequences incorporate questions addressing seven skills, the first three, literal, and the rest, inferential: (1) identifying basic stated information; (2) identifying key detail(s); (3) identifying a stated relationship; (4) inferring a simple implied relationship; (5) inferring a complex implied relationship; (6) inferring an author's generalization about the world outside a work from the work; and (7) making structural generalizations.

Chapter 2. Enabling Critical Conversation

1. For a full discussion of these issues and their classroom implications, see Bill Corcoran's excellent article, "Spiders, Surgeons and Anxious Aliens: Three Classroom Allies" (1988).

2. In "Let's Get Rid of the Welfare Mess in the Teaching of Writing," (1984) Donald Graves notes that "most teaching of writing is set up to make the writer dependent on the teacher" (43). When teachers exercise complete control over all phases of writing, the only question left for students to ask is, "What do teachers want?" (44). Graves insists that we must return control to students.

Chapter 3. Writing Next to Texts: Dialogue Journals

1. Ann Berthoff deserves credit for popularizing these forms. In *Forming/Thinking/Writing*, she recommends that students "save the left-hand side of the open double page [in their writing journals] for notes, quotations, drawings, and what we will be calling *chaos* and *oppositions*" (1982, 49). They are then to "use the right-hand side for composing sentences and paragraphs" (49). The idea, she explains, is to "use the facing pages as a

way of representing the dialogue/dialectic of the composing process" (49).

In *The Making of Meaning*, Berthoff applies a similar strategy to teaching students to write and think about literature. Developing critical consciousness depends on being alert to the ways in which texts mediate among interpreter, symbol (language), and meaning. She suggests that personal writing serves to develop critical readers because students see the example of their own emerging texts and because such classroom writing develops the habit of reflective questioning. For Berthoff, a real power of such personal writing resides in what she labels the "interpretive paraphrase," which forces students to ask, "How does it change the meaning when I change the text . . . ?" (1981, 45).

2. The samples of student writing in this book came from my classes at Iolani School over the past few years. When citing journals, logs, or other unfinished, expressive writing, I have not used student names because, although they gave me permission to use their work, these students never revised it for public display. However, in the case of writing that was intended for an audience—work that has been handed in or published in the classroom—I felt it only proper to acknowledge authorship.

3. Many theorists from classical times to the present have dealt with the relationships between writer and audience. In recent years, the nature of those relationships has been seen anew. No longer is a writer thought of as aiming his or her message toward an existing, intimately known audience. Current theory holds that the audience of a work is as much a construction of the language of the text as are its characters or narrator. Russell Long provides a central statement of this understanding: "A writer's choice of alternatives determines his audience. . . . His decisions *create* a very specific reader who exists only for the duration of the reading experience" (1980, 222). Lisa Ede and Andrea Lunsford address this same issue in detail in a more recent essay (1984). Perhaps the diffusion and impersonalization of audience that occurred after the invention of the printing press—and that led Sartre to bemoan the loss of audience altogether (1978)—has led to this increased demand that poetic language essentially contextualize itself by generating its own vision/version of audience.

Chapter 4. Writing Through Texts: Process Logs

1. Often teachers remove category choices from student control by well-meaning (but sometimes counterproductive) assignment design. For example, when students are required to write in a particular mode (definition, analysis, argument, etc.), they are correspondingly limited in the shape

and extent of their inquiry. Assignment design must be informed; if we are going to limit choices, we must do so for carefully considered reasons. We need to be careful not to overdesign assignments too often, or we will keep students on "writer's welfare" (see note 2 in chapter 2).

Chapter 9. Sequencing Inquiry into Poetry

1. Ann Loux (1987) suggests an interesting follow-up activity to Dickinson imitations. She presents students with a Dickinson original and four student imitations, asking them to choose the original. Claiming "they always win that game," she then asks them to write "what Dickinson does that the imitations could not, or tell how they recognized the original" (467). Student observations provide the basis for insightful class discussion.

Works Cited

Abercrombie, Minnie J. 1960. *The Anatomy of Judgment.* New York: Basic Books.

Anderson, Chris. 1988. "Essay Hearsay Evidence and Second–Class Citizenship." *College English* 50. 3:300–308.

Applebee, Arthur N. 1981. *Writing in the Secondary School: English and the Content Areas.* Urbana, Ill.: National Council of Teachers of English.

Barnet, Sylvan. 1985. *A Short Guide to Writing about Literature.* Boston and Toronto: Little, Brown.

Bartholomae, David. 1983. "Writing Assignments: Where Writing Begins." In *Fforum: Essays on Theory and Practice in the Teaching of Writing.* Patricia L. Stock, ed. Portsmouth, N.H.: Boynton/Cook.

Berkenkotter, Carol. 1981. "Understanding a Writer's Awareness of Audience." *College Composition and Communication* 32: 388–99.

Berlin, James A., and Robert P. Inkster. 1980. "Current-Traditional Rhetoric: Paradigm and Practice." *Freshman English News* 8.4: 1–4, 13–14.

Berthoff, Ann E. 1981. *The Making of Meaning: Metaphors, Models, and Maxims for Writing Teachers.* Portsmouth, N.H.: Boynton/Cook, 1981.

———. 1982. *Forming/Thinking/Writing: The Composing Imagination.* Portsmouth, N.H.: Boynton/Cook.

Bishop, Elizabeth. 1969. *The Complete Poems.* New York: Farrar, Straus and Giroux.

Bleich, David. 1975. *Readings and Feelings.* Urbana, Ill.: National Council of Teachers of English.

———. 1978. *Subjective Criticism.* Baltimore: Johns Hopkins University Press.

Bloom, Benjamin S., ed. 1956. *Taxonomy of Educational Objectives: Handbook I: Cognitive Domain.* New York: David McKay.

Bloom, Harold. 1973. *The Anxiety of Influence: A Theory of Poetry.* New York: Oxford University Press.

———. 1975. *A Map of Misreading.* New York: Oxford University Press.

Brittin, Norman A., and Ruth L. Brittin, eds. 1986. *A Writing Apprenticeship.* 5th ed. New York: Holt, Rinehart & Winston.

Bruffee, Kenneth A. 1984. "Collaborative Learning and the 'Conversation of Mankind.' " *College English* 46: 635–52.

Bruner, Jerome S. 1957. "On Perceptual Readiness." *Psychological Review* 64: 123–52.

Burke, Kenneth. 1966. *Language as Symbolic Action: Essays on Life, Literature and Method.* Berkeley, Los Angeles, London: University of California Press.

Christensen, Francis. 1983. "A Generative Rhetoric of the Sentence." In *Theory and Practice in the Teaching of Composition: Processing, Distancing, and Modeling.* Miles Myers and James Gray, eds. Urbana, Ill.: National Council of Teachers of English.

Cohen, B. Bernard. 1973. *Writing about Literature.* Glenview, Ill.: Scott, Foresman.

Corbett, Edward P. J. [1965] 1971. *Classical Rhetoric for the Modern Student.* New York: Oxford University Press.

Corcoran, Bill. 1988. "Spiders, Surgeons, and Anxious Aliens: Three Classroom Allies." *English Journal* 77.1: 39–44.

Crews, Frederick. 1984. *The Random House Handbook.* 4th ed. New York: Random House.

Culler, Jonathan. 1980. "Literary Competence." In *Reader-Response Criticism: From Formalism to Post-Structuralism.* Jane Tompkins, ed. Baltimore: Johns Hopkins University Press.

Davis, Robert Con, ed. 1986. *Contemporary Literary Criticism: Modernism Through Poststructuralism.* New York and London: Longman.

Dickens, Charles. 1973. *Great Expectations.* New York: Washington Square Press.

Ede, Lisa, and Andrea Lunsford. 1984. "Audience Addressed/Audience Invoked: The Role of Audience in Composition Theory and Pedagogy." *College Composition and Communication* 35: 155–71.

Elbow, Peter. 1985. "The Shifting Relationships Between Speech and Writing." *College Composition and Communication* 36: 283–303.

———. 1986. *Embracing Contraries: Explorations in Learning and Teaching.* New York and Oxford: Oxford University Press.

Eliot, T. S. 1932. "The Function of Criticism." In *Selected Essays*. New York: Harcourt, Brace.

———. 1964. *The Sacred Wood: Essays on Poetry and Criticism*. London: Methuen.

Emig, Janet. [1977] 1983. "Writing as a Mode of Learning." *College Composition and Communication* 28: 122–128. Reprinted in *The Web of Meaning: Essays on Writing, Teaching, Learning, and Thinking*. 1983. Dixie Goswami and Maureen Butler, eds. Portsmouth, N.H.: Boynton/Cook.

Fahnestock, Jeanne, and Marie Secor. 1983. "Teaching Argument: A Theory of Types." *College Composition and Communication* 34: 20–30.

Fish, Stanley. 1980. "Literature in the Reader: Affective Stylistics." In *Reader-Response Criticism: From Formalism to Post Structuralism*. Jane Tompkins, ed. Baltimore: Johns Hopkins University Press.

———. 1986. "Interpreting the *Variorum*." In *Contemporary Literary Criticism: Modernism Through Poststructuralism*. Robert Con Davis, ed. New York and London: Longman.

Franklin, Benjamin. 1985. "From *The Autobiography*." In *The American Tradition in Literature*, 6th ed. George Perkins, Sculley Bradley, Richmond Croom Beatty, and E. Hudson Long, eds. New York: Random House.

Frye, Northrop. 1970. *The Stubborn Structure: Essays on Criticism and Society*. Ithaca, N.Y.: Cornell University Press.

Gibson, Walker. 1983. "Hearing Voices: Tough Talk, Sweet Talk, Stuffy Talk." In *Theory and Practice in the Teaching of Composition: Processing, Distancing, and Modeling*. Miles Myers and James Gray, eds. Urbana, Ill.: National Council of Teachers of English.

Gordon, Edward J. 1973. *Writing about Imaginative Literature*. New York: Harcourt Brace Jovanovich.

Graves, Donald H. 1984. "Let's Get Rid of the Welfare Mess in the Teaching of Writing." In *A Researcher Learns to Write: Selected Articles and Monographs*. Portsmouth, N.H.:Heinemann.

Griffin, John Howard. 1976. *Black Like Me*. New York: Signet.

Hairston, Maxine. 1982. "The Winds of Change: Thomas Kuhn and the Revolution in the Teaching of Writing." *College Composition and Communication* 33: 76–88.

Hillocks, George, Jr., and Larry Ludlow. 1984. "A Taxonomy of Skills in Reading and Interpreting Fiction." *American Educational Research Journal* 21.1: 7–24.

Holland, Norman N. 1975. *Five Readers Reading*. New Haven and London: Yale University Press.

Holman, C. Hugh. 1972. *A Handbook to Literature*. 3rd ed. Indianapolis: Bobbs-Merrill.

Iser, Wolfgang. 1986. "The Reading Process: A Phenomenological Approach." In *Contemporary Literary Criticism: Modernism Through Poststructuralism*. Robert Con Davis, ed. New York and London: Longman.

Joyce, James. 1964. *A Portrait of the Artist as a Young Man*. New York: Viking Press.

———. 1986. *Ulysses*. Hans Walter Gabler, ed., with Wolfhard Steppe and Claus Melchior. New York: Vintage Books.

Kahn, Elizabeth A., Carolyn Calhoun Walter and Larry R. Johannessen. 1984. *Writing about Literature*. Urbana, Ill.: National Council of Teachers of English and ERIC.

Kroll, Barry M. 1984. "Writing for Readers: Three Perspectives on Audience." *College Composition and Communication* 35: 172–85.

Lauer, Janice M. 1982. "Writing as Inquiry: Some Questions for Teachers." *College Composition and Communication* 33: 89–93.

Long, Russell C. 1980. "Writer-Audience Relationships: Analysis or Invention." *College Composition and Communication* 31: 221–26.

Loux, Ann. 1987. "Using Imitations in Literature Classes." *College Composition and Communication* 38: 466–72.

McCrimmon, James M. 1984. *Writing with a Purpose*. 8th ed. Joseph F. Trimmer and Nancy I. Sommers, eds. Boston: Houghton Mifflin.

Miller, J. Hillis. 1968. *The Form of Victorian Fiction*. Notre Dame and London: University of Notre Dame Press.

Moffett, James. 1981. *Active Voice: A Writing Program Across the Curriculum*. Portsmouth, N.H.: Boynton/Cook.

———. 1983. *Teaching the Universe of Discourse*. Portsmouth, N.H.: Boynton/Cook.

———. 1988. *Coming on Center: Essays in English Education*. 2nd ed. Portsmouth, N.H.: Boynton/Cook.

Murray, Donald M. 1986. "Reading While Writing." In *Only Connect: Uniting Reading and Writing*. Thomas Newkirk, ed. Portsmouth, N.H.: Boynton/Cook.

Myers, Miles, and James Gray, eds. 1983. *Theory and Practice in the Teaching of Composition: Processing, Distancing, and Modeling*. Urbana, Ill.: National Council of Teachers of English.

Newkirk, Thomas. 1990. "Looking for Trouble: A Way to Unmask Our Readings." In *To Compose: Teaching Writing in High School and College*. 2nd ed. Thomas Newkirk, ed. Portsmouth, N.H.: Heinemann.

Petrosky, Anthony R. 1982. "From Story to Essay: Reading and Writing." *College Composition and Communication* 33: 19–36.

———. 1986. "Critical Thinking: Qu'est-ce que c'est?" *The English Record of the New York State English Council: Reading/Writing/Thinking/Learning* 37.3: 2–5.

Poulet, George. 1986. "Phenomenology of Reading." in *Contemporary Literary Criticism: Modernism Through Poststructuralism.* Robert Con Davis, ed. New York and London: Longman.

Prince, Gerald. 1980. "Introduction to the Study of the Narratee." In *Reader-Response Criticism: From Formalism to Post-Structuralism.* Jane Tompkins, ed. Baltimore: Johns Hopkins University Press.

Richards, I. A. 1958. *How to Read a Page.* Boston: Beacon Press.

Roberts, Edgar V. 1983. *Writing Themes about Literature.* Englewood Cliffs, N.J.: Prentice-Hall.

Rosenblatt, Louise M. 1978. *The Reader, the Text, the Poem: The Transactional Theory of the Literary Work.* Carbondale and Edwardsville: Southern Illinois University Press; London and Amsterdam: Feffer & Simons.

Sartre, Jean-Paul. 1978. *What Is Literature?* Trans. Bernard Frechtman. Gloucester, Mass.: Peter Smith.

Scardamalia, Marlene. 1984. "Higher Order Abilities: Written Communication." ERIC. ED 273 573.

Scholes, Robert. 1985. *Textual Power: Literary Theory and the Teaching of English.* New Haven and London: Yale University Press.

Shaler, Nathaniel Southgate. [1962] 1967. "How Agassiz Taught Shaler." In *Toward Liberal Education.* Louis G. Locke, William M. Gibson, and George Arms, eds. New York: Holt, Rinehart & Winston.

Smith, Frank. 1988. *Joining the Literacy Club: Further Essays into Education.* Portsmouth, N.H.: Heinemann.

Stallman, R. W. 1976. "Stephen Crane: A Revaluation." In *The Red Badge of Courage: An Authorative Text.* 2nd ed. Sculley Bradley, Richmond Croom Beatty, E. Hudson Long, and Donald Pizer, eds. New York: W. W. Norton.

Stevenson, Robert Louis. 1906. *Memories and Portraits.* 13th ed. London: Chatto & Windus.

Stock, Patricia L., ed. 1983. *Fforum: Essays on Theory and Practice in the Teaching of Writing.* Portsmouth, N.H.: Boynton/Cook.

Stoppard, Tom. 1967. *Rosencrantz and Guildenstern Are Dead.* New York: Grove Press.

Tompkins, Jane, ed. 1980. *Reader-Response Criticism: From Formalism to Post-Structuralism.* Baltimore: Johns Hopkins University Press.

Vygotsky, Lev. 1986. *Thought and Language.* Alex Kozulin, trans. and ed. Cambridge, Mass., and London: The MIT Press.

Williams, William Carlos. 1986. "The Crab and the Box." In *An Introduction to Poetry*. 6th ed. X. J. Kennedy, ed. Boston and Toronto: Little, Brown.

Wolff, Cynthia Griffin. 1986. *Emily Dickinson*. New York: Alfred A. Knopf.

Woolf, Virginia. 1929. *A Room of One's Own*. San Diego, New York, and London: Harcourt Brace Jovanovich.

Index